The Holy Spirit
in
THE BOOK
of
Common Prayer

John W. Wesley

WESTBOW·
PRESS
A DIVISION OF THOMAS NELSON
& ZONDERVAN

New Revised Standard Version Bible, copyright © 1989, Division of Christian Education of the National Council of the Churches of Christ in the United States of America. Used by permission. All rights reserved.

Scripture taken from the New King James Version. Copyright © 1979, 1980, 1982 by Thomas Nelson, Inc. Used by permission. All rights reserved.

WestBow Press books may be ordered through booksellers or by contacting:

WestBow Press
A Division of Thomas Nelson & Zondervan
1663 Liberty Drive
Bloomington, IN 47403
www.westbowpress.com
1 (866) 928-1240

Because of the dynamic nature of the Internet, any web addresses or links contained in this book may have changed since publication and may no longer be valid. The views expressed in this work are solely those of the author and do not necessarily reflect the views of the publisher, and the publisher hereby disclaims any responsibility for them.

Any people depicted in stock imagery provided by Thinkstock are models, and such images are being used for illustrative purposes only. Certain stock imagery © Thinkstock.

ISBN: 978-1-4908-6880-6 (sc)
ISBN: 978-1-4908-6881-3 (hc)
ISBN: 978-1-4908-6879-0 (e)

Library of Congress Control Number: 2015902941

Print information available on the last page.

WestBow Press rev. date: 02/23/2015

Contents

FOREWORD

As a pastor of many years, often in small, struggling parishes, Father John Wesley has been at work in the Episcopal vineyard since "early in the morning" and has "borne the burden of the work and the heat of the day." He can, then, help us—we who have perhaps been "loitering in the market place" and have come to the harvest late or lackadaisically—to find where the ripest grapes are clustered.

We may not at first be eager for the hard work, but his intensity of focus and faith may make us take a deep breath and square our shoulders, resolving to work harder to begin a deeper life empowered by the Holy Spirit. He understands that we may find it easier to deify sports heroes like Michael Jordan and *want to be like Mike*, but persons who *want to be like Christ* need something more than special athletic shoes; *they need the Holy Spirit.*

Father Wesley supposes many of us may have a stronger connection to the Father and Son than we do to the Holy Spirit, but believes access to the *power of the Holy Spirit* is not far away. It is embodied eloquently in the prayers and rituals of *The Book of Common Prayer*. He documents key passages and asks us to attend intensely, to hear and see more deeply what the promised gifts and treasures of the Spirit are. He dares to assume that ordinary people like you and I can and will intend a more profound purposefulness in participating in the liturgy and sacraments and that we can and will ask for, expect, receive, savor, and live out the special energies and gifts flowing from the Holy Spirit. Essentially, word by word, phrase by phrase, he finds it all spelled out in the Prayer Book. We need only ask the Spirit to awaken us to the riches of our faith and to empower us to *really believe what we believe we believe.*

No matter that the church may seem in decline or that our culture may be losing trust in institutions and organized religion, no matter that religious historians suggest that we are in the midst of a paradigm shift, living in a time of necessary reassessment and change (it happens about every 500 years, they say). Father Wesley acknowledges and confronts the crisis but thinks the solution is close at hand, hidden in plain sight. *The Book of Common Prayer* continues to be trustworthy and loved; it embodies the essentials of Scripture, reason, and tradition. Most importantly, it explicitly invites us again and again into vital relationship with the Holy Spirit.

In our Alabama diocese, the bishop has urged us to "Hold fast to that which is good/and sing a new song unto the Lord." Father Wesley's book suggests that the specific words of *The Book of Common Prayer* are surely among the treasured "things that are good," and that a "new song" can be sung simply by living more deeply into its meaning and promises. The Prayer Book's words relating to the Holy Spirit are themselves somehow timeless lyrics, an *always new song* promising the Spirit's empowering of ordinary people "to respect the dignity of every human being," "to seek and serve Christ in all persons," and to follow "a more excellent way" as members of the mystical body and the family of God.

John Wesley has been my pastor in the past and will be my friend always in the future. I have learned from his sure and sturdy faith.

—James Mersmann

DEDICATION

I dedicate this book to all faithful Episcopalians who love their church as I do and yearn to see our church once again growing strong, and maybe most importantly, making a difference in the increasingly chaotic society in which we live.

The New Revised Standard Version of the Bible has been used exclusively, unless otherwise noted.

For the purposes of this book, *The 1979 American Book of Common Prayer* has been used exclusively, and has been certified by the Church Publishing Company as public domain.

INTRODUCTION

An ordained Episcopal priest for over forty years, I grieve, as I'm sure many others do as well, over the steady decline of our church in membership, stature, and influence. Many have simply left the denomination, laying the blame for our decline on moral apathy spawned by theological liberalism and biblical revisionism. Some at the other end of the continuum fault our cumbersome institutions and outdated traditions, claiming they are no longer relevant to a "postmodern society."[1] The biggest problem with both of these theories about the cause of our current predicament is that neither offers a solution, other than leaving or radically reinventing the Episcopal Church.

I would like in this book to offer another solution. *Let's rediscover the religious and spiritual tradition we already have,* as laid out for us in *The American Book of Common Prayer,* especially the element of our tradition with which we are possibly the least familiar: *the Holy Spirit.*

I have selected this focus for two reasons. First, the Holy Spirit is the person of the Trinity with whom Episcopalian laypeople seem to be the least familiar. Second, as I will develop at length in Chapter 1, throughout *The Book of Common Prayer* and in both Old and New Testaments, the Holy Spirit is spoken of and

---

[1]   *Webster's* online dictionary defines post modernism as "a theory that involves a radical reappraisal of modern assumptions about culture, identity, history, or language."

revealed to be "the power of God at work in the Church and the world" (BCP, p. 852, lines 16 and 17).

It seems logical, therefore, that if we fail to develop a useable knowledge of the Holy Spirit, we have also inadvertently overlooked the dynamic source of spiritual *power* that *The Book of Common Prayer*, in total agreement with the New Testament, identifies as "God at work in the world and in the Church even now" (BCP. p. 852). It may seem overly dramatic to claim that, as a result, we have become a *disempowered* church. However, a closer look at the radical decline in numbers, income, and influence during the first decade of the twenty-first century should convince us that it really is true. We have lost track of the source of our spiritual power, and it is only logical to assume the decline will continue until we get reconnected.

Dr. Elizabeth Dreyer [2] puts it this way: "How deeply do we live and teach the truth that Baptism confers *the* distinctive hallmark of the Christian life – possession of the Spirit of Christ? … If we do not have the tools or the will to allow the Spirit to operate in visible, explicitly named ways, the Spirit remains silent and invisible. Without the Spirit, our exercise of discipleship, leadership and power remains hollow" (Dreyer, p. 256).

Movements like the charismatic movement in the late 1960s and beyond found little appeal among the majority of Episcopalians, partly because of the eventual focus resting on such phenomena of the Spirit as speaking in tongues, being *slain* in the Spirit, prophetic utterance, and exorcism. This focus actually seemed to have an opposing effect on our denomination rather than providing a stimulus to reignite the fire of the Spirit in the body of the Episcopal Church. And, in a sort of baby out with the

---

[2] Elizabeth A. Dreyer, *Holy Power, Holy Presence* (Mahwah, NJ: Paulist Press, 2007). See pp. 256–260 for the longer context of her quotation.

bathwater reaction, the *empowerment* that normally accompanies the Spirit was lost as well.

So, I ask you the reader, are you ready to take a new and more balanced look at the Spirit, and do it using the contents of the source with which we Episcopalians are most familiar—*The Book of Common Prayer*? You might be surprised to discover not only a renewed understanding of the third person of the Holy Trinity, but to rediscover a connection with the Spirit's accompanying *power* as well.

My hope is that everyone who reads this book will see in a renewed way the dramatic role the Holy Spirit plays in all of the rites and prayers in *The American Book of Common Prayer* and will become as convinced as I am that the Holy Spirit is the solution to our denomination's current power crisis. By looking again at the Holy Spirit as he is named, acknowledged, invoked, and applied in our own *Book of Common Prayer*, I believe we can also find in our Prayer Book ways of accessing the power of the Holy Spirit for personal, congregational, denominational, and social benefit. If these things can happen, then I believe we will experience a reigniting of the flame that once made our denomination great. It is that hope that propels me to write this book.

So, beginning with the theme of the Holy Spirit as the *power* of God, let us set out to explore what insights our *American Book of Common Prayer* might hold.

CHAPTER 1

The Holy Spirit as the Power of God

> May the God of hope fill you with all joy and peace
> in believing, so that by the power of the Holy Spirit
> you may abound in hope.
>
> —Romans 15:13

My goal in this first chapter is to create in your mind an association that may not already exist. By the end of this chapter, when you hear or read the words *Holy Spirit*, I would like you to think of the power of God. Say it over to yourself a few times right now: Holy Spirit, power of God; Holy Spirit, power of God. Allow the association to become cemented in your brain: the Holy Spirit is the power of God.

The idea of spiritual power may conjure images of the dramatic supernatural occurrences that defined the ministry of Jesus as he went about curing lepers, casting out demonic spirits, and walking on water. If it is this association that has entered your mind, it would seem almost natural for you to conclude, "Well, if that kind of thing happens at all anymore, it is for other people, certainly not for me. After all, I'm just an ordinary person." But my question is this: are there other associations with the term *spiritual power* that might be more relatable for ordinary people like us?

Dr. Lois Malcolm is a Lutheran pastor and a professor at Luther Theological Seminary in St. Paul, Minnesota. In her most recent book, Dr. Malcolm affirms resolutely that the Holy Spirit is a source of creative power accessible to anyone, and it can be harnessed to help us do relatively ordinary things more effectively. She says, "Living in the Spirit is precisely about living out of God's creative power in our own lives. The Spirit is God's energizing power in our lives."[3]

What if by rethinking our ideas about the power of the Holy Spirit, we were able to see it as something God intends ordinary people like us to tap into as a source of spiritual strength to accomplish the things we are called upon to do? Would you like to be a more effective Sunday school teacher, a more helpful greeter, or a more discerning vestry member? What if you could become a more satisfied pray-er, a more fruitful student of Scripture, or a more comforting Christian friend? What if you could accomplish more in the outreach projects you are passionate about and to which you already devote your own time and energy? It is this spiritual power—divinely provided for every Christian—that transforms our relatively ordinary actions into extraordinary successes.

As an Episcopal clergy person for the past forty-plus years, I am troubled to see our denomination struggling as it is, with many congregations barely surviving and their members experiencing all the feelings of guilt and discouragement that accompany just hanging on. I know that I'm not the only person praying and hoping for some kind of improvement, while seeing few apparent changes. But here is what my mind keeps flashing back to:

- If churches exist to do the work of God in the world, and

---

[3] Lois Malcolm, *Holy Spirit: Creative Power in Our Lives* (Minneapolis, Minnesota: Augsburg Press, 2009), 61.

- If the God we serve is that same God of the universe who spoke every created thing into being, then
- Isn't it logical to believe God wants his churches to thrive and be effective, and that he will ably supply the power to help them do that?

One of the things that often accompanies congregational discouragement is personal self-doubt. Both clergy and laypersons are capable of feeling there must be something wrong with them. I'm not trying to be flippant when I suggest that feeling inadequate seems to be almost a precondition when God sets out to find people to be part of his work. He frequently seems to use people who are reluctant to be used and who feel woefully inadequate for whatever tasks God may call them to perform.

Moses complained he was not eloquent. When David considered that he was the youngest in his family, from the smallest tribe of Israel, and that his only work experience was as a shepherd, he naturally assumed he could be of no use to God. Jeremiah also thought of himself as too young to be useful, while Isaiah was certain God would not use someone as sinful as he thought himself to be. Joseph, Daniel, and Nehemiah were slaves. Many of Jesus' disciples were what one hymnist calls humble fisher folk. Nonetheless, God did call on all of these (and many others), and he empowered them to do the work he wanted them to do.

So, I would like to invite you to think of spiritual power in a new way. Try not to think of the giant and dramatic miracles of Jesus and the saints. Try to think instead of ordinary Christians like yourselves doing relatively ordinary things but doing them more effectively because of the spiritual power promised by God, which is accessible to all Christians. Repeat this thought to yourself whenever you begin to doubt that God will empower you to do his work: *He wants to use people like me. I recognize and acknowledge my human limitations but am willing to let God empower me to accomplish his work.*

When I began to apply this principle to my own ministry, I saw two things to be true. First, I could see that God had, in fact, given me certain natural skills. But, second, I could also see it was the Holy Spirit's empowering me in the use of these skills that got the kind of results God was looking for in me.

I am a decent public speaker, but it has not been my natural eloquence that God uses to make a difference in people's lives. The sermons I am aware of in which something I said seemed to make a real difference in someone else's life came from *outside* of myself. I would be speaking and suddenly, words I don't remember thinking would be coming out of my mouth. And a short while later, one of the listeners would say, "That was exactly what I needed to hear."

Likewise, I think of myself as an apt teacher. But in teaching—in Sunday school, confirmation classes, adult forums, or church workshops—the times when people have told me that I made the greatest difference in their lives usually happened when someone asked an unexpected question, and we wandered off together in a new direction of Spirit-led thinking and learning. Similarly, the times when I think I have been most helpful to some other person were encounters that happened, more often than not, when I was on my way to do something else. Circumstances, one might say, got arranged by the Spirit. All I had to do was be willing to listen and to go where the Spirit was leading.

What seemed to make the difference was this: times when I learned from someone I had preached to, taught, or done something truly helpful for were times I had begun with an acknowledgment of my own inadequacy. This was accompanied by a simple, prayerful request to God to send his Holy Spirit to empower my natural abilities and achieve results greater than I could have expected. When I say a simple, prayerful request, I mean a prayer that goes something like this:

> Lord, I am not worthy to serve you; in and of myself, I have neither the wisdom nor the strength to do your work. But I know that you are a God who can and will empower me to do those things that you want done. I know that you will guide me in the right direction, give me the right words to say, and grant me the necessary sensitivity to all to whom you send me to minister. In Jesus' name, amen.

So, first of all, let me reiterate that, for me, to talk about the empowerment of the Holy Spirit is to talk about spiritual power that is available to *all* of us.

Elizabeth Dreyer[4] expresses a rather strong belief about this. She says that New Testament texts about the Holy Spirit refer to a "complex experiential field in which power is transmitted and exchanged. The *pneuma*[5] *is* precisely active power."

But, to help us get started in a process to deepen our understanding of the Holy Spirit, let us look at some places in the Prayer Book where the phrase "the power of the Holy Spirit" occurs.

---

[4]   Dreyer, op. cit., 260.

[5]   *Pneuma* is the Greek word usually translated as "Spirit" in the New Testament; it is also variously translated "breeze," "wind," and "air," like in Jesus' conversation with Nicodemus in John 3:6–8.

++ The Power of the Holy Spirit ++

Probably the most familiar occurrences of the phrase *the power of the Holy Spirit* are those in the creeds that refer to the Holy Spirit being the power that made certain events possible in the life of Jesus.

1. In the Apostles' Creed (recited in morning and evening prayer), we say that Jesus Christ "was conceived by the power of the Holy Spirit" (*Book of Common Prayer* or BCP, p. 96).

   This is also the wording used in the question and answer form of the Apostles' Creed called the baptismal covenant (BCP, p. 304).

   In the Nicene Creed (said during the celebration of Holy Communion in both Rite I and Rite II, BCP, pp. 326 and 358), we repeat the similar phrase: "By the power of the Holy Spirit he became incarnate from the Virgin Mary and was made man."

2. *Proper Prefaces* are words appropriate to the day or liturgical[6] season, spoken by the celebrant, leading into and in part explaining why we are saying "holy, holy, holy" in the service of the Holy Eucharist. These proper prefaces are found in our Prayer Book on pages 344–349 (Rite I) and pages 377–381 (Rite II). The Preface for

---

6   Within the Episcopal/Anglican tradition, we celebrate six seasons of the Christian year that we refer to as liturgical because they are part of the structured way in which we worship. The six seasons are: Advent, Christmas, and Epiphany; Lent, Easter, and Pentecost.

the Incarnation (Christmas, BCP, p. 378) contains these words:

> … Jesus Christ … who, by the mighty power of the Holy Spirit, was made perfect man …

These references probably do not surprise us, however; for it is generally easier for us to believe that God's power was at work in Jesus' life than it is for us to believe his power has been, is and will be at work in *our* lives.

So let us now turn in *The Book of Common Prayer* to some of the numerous occurrences of the phrase "the power of the Holy Spirit" in which impact on our lives is the issue.

++ The Phrase "The Power of the Holy Spirit" Referring to Followers of Jesus ++

My main concern in all of the following references—numbers three through five—is for you the reader to begin to see that there are numerous references to "the power of the Holy Spirit" that apply to all of us ordinary Christians by virtue of the fact that we have been baptized.

3. The Absolution [pronouncement by the priest after our Confession, declaring God's mercy and forgiveness] in Morning Prayer Rite II (BCP, p. 80), Evening Prayer Rite II (BCP, p. 117), Holy Eucharist Rite II (BCP, p. 353 and 360), in Communion Under Special Circumstances (BCP, p. 398), and in Ministration to the Sick (BCP, p. 455) contains these words:

"Almighty God ... by the power of the Holy Spirit keep you in eternal life."

Each time we hear these words of Absolution, we are being encouraged to think back to our baptism and to the graces conveyed in baptism which include (1) that we became inheritors of the kingdom of God (Catechism, BCP, p. 858) and (2) that we are "sealed as Christ's own forever" (BCP, p. 308). Those references indicate, as radical as it may sound, that our *eternity* begins the moment we are baptized. The Absolution, then, becomes a reminder that the Holy Spirit is the power by which we are *kept* in the eternity we already in certain ways inhabit.

4. The Proper Preface for the Incarnation, cited earlier (BCP, pp. 345 and 378), also refers back to our own baptism, specifically stating that one purpose for Jesus being born into our world was so that we might ... receive power to become [God's] children.

   This statement is consistent with the Catechism which says, in answer to the question, what is Holy Baptism?:

   Holy Baptism is the sacrament by which God adopts us as his children (BCP, p. 858).

   So again, when we hear the words of the Proper Preface for the *Incarnation*, the intention is that we be consciously reminded of our baptism, through which we became children of God *by the power of the Holy Spirit*.

The Exhortation[7] (BCP, p. 316) also specifically connects the power by which we become God's children with the Holy Spirit, stating:

"Our Savior Christ ... humbled himself even to death on the cross, that he might ... make us the children of God by the power of the Holy Spirit."

So we see that the words of the Proper Preface for the *Incarnation* and the words used in the Exhortation encourage us to reflect back on the graces conveyed to us in our baptism, specifically to the thrilling reality that, at the moment of our baptism, we ... became ... God's ... children.

It's as if a "still small voice" speaks through the words of the Exhortation and the Proper Preface to say remember that moment and savor it; enjoy its blessings and live out its implications. You *are* a child of God.

5. We find that the power of the Holy Spirit is also connected with the calling of all baptized followers of Christ to serve him as a "royal priesthood."[8]

In the proper preface for Pentecost (BCP, p. 380), reference is made to the Holy Spirit coming "down from heaven ... giving to your Church the power to serve you as a royal priesthood."

---

[7] The exhortation to examine oneself carefully before receiving Holy Communion is only infrequently used in most churches and not used at all in some. Its intention is to call us to awareness of the need to be in complete unity with other members of the body of Christ (see 1 Corinthians 11:27–32).

[8] Terminology "royal priesthood" comes from 1 Peter 2:5, 9.

The congregation voices the following invitation to the newly-baptized person:

"We receive you into the household of God. ... Share with us in [Christ's] eternal priesthood" (BCP, p. 308).

More will be said about this in the next chapter where we examine "sealing by the Holy Spirit," not only as one of the graces conveyed in Baptism, but as a grace which is directly connected to our call to participate in the "royal priesthood of Christ."

+ + Summary Thoughts + +

My hope is that I have provided sufficient documentation for you, the reader, to begin to be convinced of at least the following four important ideas:

- First, the idea of spiritual power, when used in *The American Book of Common Prayer*, is always a reference to the Holy Spirit, because "the Holy Spirit *is* the power of God at work in the Church and in the world;" (BCP, p. 852)
- Second, the references to *empowerment* by the Holy Spirit are intended for us to understand they are not only referring to Jesus being given power by the Holy Spirit to do certain things, but that we *ordinary* humans also receive the power of the Holy Spirit;
- Third, this empowerment of us begins at the moment of our baptism, even though we are not yet conscious of it;
- Fourth, in the New Testament writings of both Luke (Acts of the Apostles and the gospel of Luke) and Paul

(especially Romans and Ephesians), the Holy Spirit is specifically connected with the word and the concept of spiritual power.[9]

The next chapter will look specifically at the role of the Holy Spirit in the baptismal service and will take a deeper look at the issue of the spiritual empowerment given us in baptism.

But now, I invite and encourage you to devote some time to the following questions for thought, possibly journaling, or small group discussion.

Questions for Further Thought or Discussion

1. Day One   When you hear yourself say, "God wants to use people like me. I recognize and acknowledge my human limitations, but am willing to let God empower me to accomplish his work," how do you feel (frightened, indifferent, excited and energized, or something else)?

                What will you plan as your next step to keep moving toward greater empowerment as a follower of Christ?

2. Day Two   In your personal experience in the church, where has the power of the Holy Spirit been most evident? With what results?

---

[9]   For examples, see Luke 4:14 and 24:49; Acts 1:8; Romans 15:13, 19; and Ephesians 3:20.

3. Day Three   Have you noticed the words in the absolution that say "the power of the Holy Spirit keep you in eternal life?" If so, what have you thought those words meant? Describe what it is like for you to think of yourself as in eternity right now?

4. Day Four   Why do you think church leaders and thinkers have spent so much time trying to explain that Jesus is completely human and is also completely divine. In what ways (if any) does that reality influence your personal spirituality? (Read Hebrews 4:15–16.)

5. Day Five   "You *are* a child of God." How do you feel hearing these words? What difference does knowing these words to be true make in your life at the present time?

6. Day Six   When you hear that the Holy Spirit came "down from heaven ... giving to your Church the power to serve you as a royal priesthood" (BCP, p. 380, Proper Preface for Pentecost), what do these words mean to you? What do you see yourself doing differently as part of Christ's royal priesthood?

CHAPTER 2

The Holy Spirit as the Power of God in the Service of Holy Baptism

> How deeply do we live and teach the truth
> that Baptism Confers the distinctive hallmark of the
> Christian Life – possession of the Spirit of Christ?
> —Elizabeth Dreyer, *Holy Power, Holy Presence*

In the last chapter, we examined multiple examples in *The American Book of Common Prayer* where the power of God and the person of the Holy Spirit are presented as synonymous. The case was put forth that when God wants to get something done, he sends the Holy Spirit. In this chapter, I want to connect these ideas with our Episcopal practice and understanding of baptism.

Baptism marks the start of our Christian life; and as we shall soon see, the Holy Spirit plays a critical role in this beginning. There are principally two ways in which the Holy Spirit plays a role in baptism.

- First, the Holy Spirit is called upon to sanctify and make effective the water of baptism.
- Second, we shall note that, according to Episcopal theology of baptism, certain things are expected to happen to and for the person (usually an infant) being baptized.

After listing all the graces for which the Holy Spirit is invoked in holy baptism, Daniel Stevick concludes simply, "Baptism, according to the Prayer Book tradition, is a Spirit-filled event."[10]

Possibly the most dramatic example of the Holy Spirit's involvement in the sacrament of baptism is found in the words spoken by the priest in the prayer of Thanksgiving over the Water: "Now sanctify this water, we pray you, by the power of your Holy Spirit" (BCP, page 307).

The verb *sanctify* means, at least, to "set apart for a sacred purpose"[11] and is also used to mean actually "making something [or someone] sacred or holy."[12] In the context of baptism, it would make little sense for sanctify to mean merely "set aside for a sacred purpose." We do that with candles, crosses, altar utensils, and vestments. But there seems to be intended here an *instrumentality* that goes beyond being "set aside," even if for a higher purpose. The precise wording conveys the notion that something is actually happening to the water: The Holy Spirit is being invoked to make the water of baptism something more than mere H2O. The words suggest a belief that some kind of change is expected; otherwise, why pray at all for the water to be sanctified?

James E. Griffiss, in his book, *The Anglican Vision,*[13] says:

The prayer book liturgies of both Baptism and Eucharist make clear that it is not in the strength

---

[10] Daniel B. Stevick, *By Water and the Word: the Scriptures of Baptism.* New York: Church Pub. Inc., 1997.67.

[11] From www.merriam-webster.com/dictionary/sanctify

[12] From dictionary.reference.com/sanctify

[13] Griffiss, James E., *The Anglican Vision,* The New Church's Teaching Series, vol. 1 (Boston: Cowley Publications, 1997), 118.

of the signs – water, bread, and wine – that God is present, but rather that the Spirit of God takes the signs and makes them holy and powerful. The Holy Spirit sanctifies the water of baptism ...   (Griffiss, op. cit., p. 118)[14]

What is God the Father seeking to accomplish when he sends the Holy Spirit to sanctify the water of baptism? Our catechism (BCP p. 857) tells us that as an "outward and visible sign of inward and spiritual grace," the sacramental element of baptism (water) becomes a "sure and certain means by which we receive that grace." It seems simply logical that if what was once mere H2O now has the capability of conveying graces to an infant being baptized, the change can only be attributed to the sanctifying action of the Holy Spirit upon it, since *that* is what has been asked for.

The next logical question would seem to be, what is the inward and spiritual grace that God the Father wishes for us to receive when he sends the Holy Spirit to sanctify and *make powerful* the water of baptism, turning it into a means of grace?

We actually find a number of answers to that question scattered throughout the *American Book of Common Prayer*—in the liturgy for baptism, itself, in the Catechism, and in various Collects and Proper Prefaces.

1. First of all, in the Prayers for the Candidate(s), (BCP, p. 305), God the Father is petitioned to "Fill [the person being baptized] with your holy and life-giving Spirit."

    To say that at the moment of our baptism we are *filled* with the Holy Spirit implies, among other things, that the

---

[14] Griffiss, James E., ibid. 118.

Spirit becomes a permanent *resident* inside of us. This in fact is the wording used in the Collect of the Holy Spirit" (BCP, p. 251), wherein God is asked to "grant that by the indwelling of your Holy Spirit we may be enlightened and strengthened for your service."

John's record of Jesus' teaching about the Holy Spirit includes the point that "he dwells with you and will be in you" (see John 14:16–17).

Paul also speaks about the indwelling Spirit. In Romans 8:11 Paul says, "If the same Spirit that raised Christ from the dead dwells in you, he … will give life to your mortal bodies also through his Spirit which dwells in you." In 1 Corinthians 3:16, Paul asks the question, "Do you not know that you are God's temple and that God's Spirit dwells in you?"

Whatever else we know or believe, we can and should rest confidently in the fact that every baptized infant now has the Spirit's presence actually living inside of them. The assumption seems to be that, if that indwelling Spirit is nurtured and encouraged to grow in influence in the child's life, the child will continue to grow and mature spiritually, especially becoming more spiritually empowered.

My youngest daughter, Kate, has always had an uncanny spiritual sensitivity, and as an adult with children of her own, continues to be a faithful worker in her church. She has made certain that her own children are being brought up in the community of faith. After some inner struggle, she decided to let her own oldest child decide for herself when (or even *if*) she would stand up to confirm her own faith. Kate called me one afternoon, elated that Michal Jane had just told her she wants to confirm her faith at the bishop's next visit.

The point of this little personal vignette is to emphasize the trust we put in the Holy Spirit's *holding power* when we commit to him the lives and faith of our children and grandchildren. For certain, we have no guarantees as our culture becomes increasingly secular, that any of our children will grow up and lay claim to the faith in which they were raised. John Westerhoff, when he was teaching at Duke, wrote a book in 1976 entitled just that, *Will Our Children Have Faith?* [15] It is about how Sunday school is done. It may be a little dated, but the title still raises a challenging question.

In short, the first grace conveyed to a child by the Spirit-powered water of holy baptism is that they are *filled* with the Holy Spirit.

2. Another aspect of the inward and spiritual grace that is conveyed in baptism is also found in the same section of prayers for the candidate(s) (BCP, p. 305). God the Father is asked to give the candidate for baptism the ability "to love others in the power of the Spirit."

    I'm reminded of Jesus' teaching about love in the Sermon on the Mount. He asks, "If you love those who love you, what reward have you? For even the tax gathers do that" (Matthew 5:46). His words suggest that those of us who consider ourselves followers of his should hold ourselves to a higher standard of love. How is that possible if we are *merely human*?

    In my lifetime, I can think of no more powerful example of love than the one we saw in the life and work

---

[15] John H. Westerhoff, *Will Our Children Have Faith?* Reference only.

of Dr. Martin Luther King Jr. He gave many provocative
sermons and speeches; but of the ones I have read, I find
his sermon given at Ebenezer Baptist Church in Atlanta
in February 1968, to be one that touches me most deeply.
As if by some precognition about his own death, he said,

> Every now and then I guess we all think
> realistically about that day when we will be
> victimized with what is life's final common
> denominator — that something we call death.
> Every now and then I ask myself, "What is it that
> I would want said?" And I leave the word to you
> this morning. If you get somebody to deliver the
> eulogy, I'd like somebody to mention that day,
> that Martin Luther King, Jr., tried to give his
> life serving others. I'd like for somebody to say
> that day, that Martin Luther King, Jr., tried to
> love somebody. I want you to say that day, that
> I tried to be right on the war question. I want
> you to be able to say that day that I did try to
> feed the hungry. I want you to be able to say that
> day that I did try in my life to clothe those who
> were naked. I want you to say, on that day, that
> I did try, in my life, to visit those who were in
> prison. I want you to say that I tried to love and
> serve humanity.[16]

That kind of love obviously goes well beyond what
our culture would consider *normal* love; and certainly
the ability to love others, measured by the example of a

---

[16] from the website http://www.mccsc.edu/~mdavis/mlk/2005/Adrian/
martin.htm

higher standard seen in the life and death of Dr. King, does not come easily or naturally. If it happens at all (as it clearly did in the life of Dr. King), it has to be a grace—a gift of the Spirit. Mere human desire, intention, and willpower alone cannot and will not generate that kind of selfless servant love. That kind of love occurs only if and when it is empowered by the Holy Spirit that has filled us at our baptism. In what I believe to be one of the most profound prayers appearing in *The American Book of Common Prayer*—in the Collect for St. James—we pray "that you will pour upon the leaders of your Church that spirit of self-denying service by which alone they may have true authority among your people" (BCP, p. 242).

So this is a second of those graces we ask to be conveyed in baptism: "Teach them to love others in the power of the Spirit."

3. In the thanksgiving over the water, it is declared that "through [the water of baptism] we are reborn by the Holy Spirit" (BCP, p. 306).

Since for those of us baptized as infants it is impossible to know what we would have been like had we not been baptized, it is virtually impossible to visualize what it means to be *reborn*. Jesus seemed to foresee this difficulty when, in his conversation with Nicodemus about being born again (John 3:3–8), he points out (v. 8) that even though you cannot see "the Spirit," it is possible to see the results of the Spirit's presence.

In 2 Corinthians 5:15–17, Paul describes the effects of what he calls the *new creation* as "living no longer for oneself alone, but for him (Jesus)."

Jesus was and is the perfect example of love that "does not insist on getting its own way" (1 Corinthians 13). His prayer in the garden of Gethsemane summarized the way he had lived his life: "Nevertheless, Father, not my will, but yours be done." Paul describes his own rebirth experience in Galatians 2:20: "I have been crucified with Christ; it is no longer I who live, but Christ who lives in me."

We are given these examples in Scripture, I believe, so we will recognize that, whatever else it means to be born again, it certainly means living out of a different core and for a different purpose.

We find in the writings of so many Saints records of their struggles with replacing self-centered desires and goals with Christ-centered ones. A lesser known saint named Poeman[17] wrote: "To throw yourself before God, not to measure your progress, to leave behind all self-will; these are the instruments for the work of the soul."

A key word here is *struggles*. For a person who has not been "reborn by the Holy Spirit," there is no struggle. Life without the Spirit is simply lived for self alone. And why not? Where would the motivation come from to live any other way? Paul segues into his great love chapter of 1 Corinthians 13 with the words (1 Corinthians 12:31b), "Let me show you a still more excellent way." In this way, Paul connects the idea of rebirth with the evidence of living a life characterized by selfless love.

This "more excellent way" is available to all baptized persons who are willing to allow the indwelling power of God's Spirit to transform them on the inside. The third

---

[17] Poeman died in Egypt in 450 A. D. (from the website http://saints.sqpn. com/saintp0d.htm)

grace conveyed in baptism is to be reborn by the Spirit, to be given a vision of the possibility of life lived for Christ rather than for self.

4. As the thanksgiving over the water continues (BCP, p. 307), the priest is instructed to touch the water as he or she says, "Now sanctify this water … by the power of your Holy Spirit, that those who here are cleansed from sin and born again … may continue in the risen life of Jesus Christ our Savior." A fourth grace conveyed through baptism is the gift of power to continue in the new, un-self-centered life expected of us by God.

A friend of mine joked after finishing running his first marathon, "Getting started wasn't so hard. It was continuing for twenty-six and two-tenths miles that was difficult."

Continuing in the life of Christ truly is the hard part, isn't it? In 1991, Michael Jordan signed a ten-year, $13.5 million dollar contract with Gatorade. In the ads that followed and on playgrounds across the world, children could be heard singing the phrase, "I want to be like Mike." Michael was extremely popular; the tune was catchy. It was considered to be one of the most successful ad campaigns ever. "I want to be like Mike."

But the New Testament challenges us with a significantly higher standard than "being like Mike." The grace of "continuing in the risen life of Christ" is closely connected with "rebirth by the Holy Spirit" mentioned above. To have the Spirit to *start* the race, but not having the spirit *to continue and finish* the race really doesn't make sense, does it? Dr. Robert D. Hughes

(School of Theology, University of the South, Sewanee, Tennessee), in his article in *The Blackwell Companion to Christian Spirituality*[18] writes: "The Holy Spirit is central to Christian spirituality and to any understanding of it. In fact, the word *spirituality* reflects the realization that the Christian life is led in the power and under the guidance of the Holy Spirit."

Remember Paul's inspiring words in Philippians 3:14: "I press on toward the goal for the prize of the upward call of God in Christ Jesus. Let all of us who value maturity be like minded."

A fourth grace conveyed to us in baptism is the power to *continue*, to keep going, to press on toward the goal of becoming like Christ.

5. Similar to the idea of continuing stated here is the idea of being *sustained,* which is expressed in the prayer said by the priest (BCP, p. 308). Immediately following the actual baptism, the priest prays, "By water and the Holy Spirit you have bestowed upon *this your servant* the forgiveness of sin, and have raised them to the new life of grace. Sustain them … in your Holy Spirit."

One definition of the verb *sustain* is to supply with sustenance, to nourish. The etymology of the word (from the Latin *sustenere*) indicates a literal meaning of "to hold up from below."[19] In Chapter 4 and Appendix D on Transformation, we will look more closely at some of

---

[18] Robert Davis Hughes III, "The Holy Spirit in Christian Spirituality," in *The Blackwell Companion to Christian Spirituality,* ed. Arthur Holder (Hoboken, New Jersey: Wiley-Blackwell Publishing), 207.

[19] *Merriam Webster Online Dictionary.*

22

the ways in which the Holy Spirit sustains us. For now, however, let us simply acknowledge that a fifth grace conveyed to us in baptism is the power of the Holy Spirit to sustain us on our spiritual journey.

6. Immediately following this prayer (to be sustained by the Holy Spirit), the priest anoints the baptized person with oil, saying: "You are sealed by the Holy Spirit in Baptism and marked as Christ's own forever" (BCP, p. 308). The reason for including this Rite of sealing in the baptismal service is important, but rarely made clear to parents and godparents and understood by few, if any, members of the congregation witnessing the baptism. In Ephesians 1:13–14, Paul writes:

> "In Christ you ... were marked with the seal of the promised Holy Spirit; this is the pledge of our inheritance toward redemption as God's own people."

And in Ephesians 4:30, Paul again makes reference to "the Holy Spirit of God, with whom you were marked with a seal for the day of redemption."

The sealing of the Holy Spirit, then, is the power by which we are *kept* in God's grace until we experience its final fulfillment in heaven.

A second explanation of the significance of our sealing is stated in the words of the prayer for consecrating the chrism (oil used for anointing in baptism and confirmation) which addresses, "Eternal Father, whose blessed Son was anointed by the Holy Spirit to be the Savior and servant of all[20], we pray you to consecrate this oil … that those who are sealed with it may share in the royal priesthood of Jesus Christ" (BCP, p. 307).

The bishop's prayer in the service of confirmation (BCP, p. 418) refers back to the charge to share in the eternal priesthood of Christ, first stated in the baptismal service as an expected outcome of being sealed by the Holy Spirit. The bishop prays to God saying, "By the sealing of your Holy Spirit you have bound us to your service … Send [these … confirmands] forth in the power of that Spirit to perform the service you set before them."

It should be noted that, while the exact connection between baptism and confirmation is still the subject of much debate, and much has been written on the subject (see Stevick[21]), suffice it to say for our purposes here that our baptismal charge to share with all Christians in the eternal priesthood of Christ is reiterated and strengthened in confirmation by the reference to empowerment given by the Holy Spirit.

The sealing by the Holy Spirit is the sixth of the important graces conveyed to us in holy baptism.

7. Just prior to transitioning into Holy Communion with the passing of the peace, the priest invites the congregation to join him or her in saying to the newly baptized, "We receive you into the household of God" (BCP, p. 308). If the intent of this comment is not clear enough,

---

[20] This prayer refers to the association made by Luke between the anointing of Jesus by the Holy Spirit and the fact that it happened at the time of his baptism (Luke 3:21ff. and 4:18; and referred to in Acts 4:27 and 10:38).

[21] Stevick, *Baptismal Moments; Baptismal Meaning,* (Chicago: Church Hymnal Corp., 2007), especially Chapter II, "Historical Development of Baptismal Rites, Ancient to Modern."

our Catechism says more specifically in answer to the question, "What is Holy Baptism?"

"Holy Baptism is the sacrament by which God adopts us as his children and ... makes us members of Christ's Body, the Church, and inheritors of the kingdom of God" (BCP, p. 858).

And, in answer to the question, "What is the inward and spiritual grace in Baptism?" the Catechism (BCP, p. 858) adds:

The inward and spiritual grace in Baptism is ... birth into God's family the Church.

Of all the graces conveyed in baptism, the one which seems under-appreciated in our day is this one: active participation in the church, being an active part of Christ's body, the church.

Robert D. Hughes' book, *Beloved Dust,* offers a number of useful insights, possibly one of the most needed today being his comments about the role of the covenant community. He ties a number of important themes together as he writes,

> Personal character is formed by a process of socialization and enculturation, not simply by the indwelling of the Holy Spirit in separate movements in one individual person after another. Indeed, the principal 'indwelling' of the Holy Spirit is in the covenant community, through its common life shaping individual persons for membership in a priestly people. Individual entrance into this community (for Christians) is normatively through the sacrament

of Baptism, which also, of course, engrafts one into the community of faith as a member of the Body of Christ, the Church ... To be in Christ, in the Spirit, is always also to be in the Church as a member of the people of God on mission. We cannot unlearn hate and learn to love by ourselves.[22]

If his words were to be taken to heart by every serious-minded Episcopalian, would we not possibly be back on the path to needed reform, but from within? That is, the Holy Spirit would transform our inner spirits to recognize and desire communion and fellowship with other Christians. In addition, his remarks segue into my final entry on the list of baptismal graces.

8. To remind us in yet another way of the connection between baptism and "active membership in the Church," the Catechism addresses the same subject from a slightly different portal, recalling to us that "Infants are baptized so they can share citizenship in the Covenant" (BCP, p. 858).

A covenant is a contractual relationship between two parties stipulating the conditions that both parties are agreeing to. In short, God the Father, from his side, agrees to give us all the graces mentioned above. The logical counterpart would seem to be that, by being baptized, we give tacit agreement to the conditions either stated or implied.

---

[22] Robert D. Hughes III, *Beloved Dust*, New York: Continuum Publishing Group, 2008, 160–161.

This covenantal obligation is spelled out in the section of the Catechism on the New Covenant and in the preceding section on God the Son (BCP, p. 850), where the victory of God the Son (Jesus) over sin, suffering, and death is mentioned, we are told, "We share in his victory when we are baptized into the New Covenant and become living members of Christ."

If I recall my church history class in seminary correctly, the Armenians, who strongly influenced Wesleyan Methodist theology, believe that if baptized persons fail to continue their active membership in the church, then God will not honor His side of the covenant by continuing to supply the graces promised. Nearly all other Christian denominational groups believe that God *always* remains faithful to his covenant promises. If we choose not to remain faithful to our side of the covenant, we may simply miss out on some of the benefits of the graces we have received. But the graces themselves, once given in baptism, are irrevocable. Romans 11:29, in many translations, including the NIV translation reads: "for God's gifts and his call are *irrevocable*" (emphasis added).

I remember when I was in college, a friend and I typically walked a few blocks to a church for early Mass. One particular Sunday, I had stayed up too late Saturday night (studying, of course) and didn't feel like rolling out of bed. My friend was persistent, however, and so I gave in. Had I not listened to my friend, I would have missed out on a sermon that I really needed to hear (not to mention a wonderful potluck lunch that we had forgotten about and meeting a couple of young ladies that seemed interested in going on a date with us. God is good!).

A composite list of the blessings and benefits received in baptism (mentioned in the above references) looks something like this:

We are *filled* with the Holy Spirit. By this filling we are:

- given the ability to love others
- reborn/born again/raised to a new life of grace
- cleansed from sin/forgiven of sin
- made able to continue in the risen life of Christ
- provided all that is necessary to be sustained in our Christian life
- sealed for eternity/made an inheritor of the kingdom of God
- adopted as God's children
- born into God's family, the church
- made living members of Christ's body, the church.

I list these multiple graces here for three reasons:

- First, I want to again emphasize the abundance of benefits conveyed in baptism.
- Second, it is my hope that, at some point in each of our lives, we would spend some time reflecting on the implications of being recipients of these abundant benefits. An important question seems to be, as beneficiaries of such astounding rewards, what kind of response from us does a reasonable God have a right to expect?

I am reminded of a passage from Peter's second letter in which he connects the "great and precious promises we have received" with the necessity of being fruitful as bearers of those gifts:

As His divine power has given to us all things that
pertain to life and godliness, through the knowledge
of Him who called us by glory and virtue, by which
have been given to us exceedingly great and precious
promises, that through these you may be partakers
of the divine nature, having escaped the corruption
that is in the world through lust. For if these things
are yours and abound, you will be neither barren nor
unfruitful in the knowledge of our Lord Jesus Christ
(2 Peter 1:3–8 NKJV).

- Last, I believe understanding these benefits is necessary
groundwork for us to understand the relevance and
importance of everything else *The American Book of
Common Prayer* says about the work of the Holy Spirit in
believers' individual lives. This subject will be dealt with
in depth in Chapter 4.

Questions for Further Thought or Discussion

1. Day One: In baptism, I was *filled* with the Holy Spirit. By
this filling I was …
   - Given the ability to love others

Question: What evidence is there that my ability to love
others has been effected by my baptism?

2. Day Two: In baptism, I was *filled* with the Holy Spirit. By
this filling I was …
   - Reborn/born again/raised to a new life of grace

Question: What evidence is there from my life that I have experienced a new life of grace?

3. Day Three: In baptism, I was *filled* with the Holy Spirit. By this filling I was …
    ▪ Cleansed from sin/forgiven of sin

    Question: In what ways has knowing that God forgives my sin made a difference in my life?

4. Day Four: In baptism, I was *filled* with the Holy Spirit. By this filling I was …
    ▪ Made able to continue in the risen life of Christ/ given everything necessary to be sustained in my Christian life

Question: In what ways have I made a conscious connection between my ability to continue living as a Christian and what happened at my baptism? What could I be doing to improve my awareness of this connection?

5. Day Five: In baptism, I was *filled* with the Holy Spirit. By this filling I was …
    ▪ Sealed for eternity/made an inheritor of the kingdom of God

    Question: In what ways would I describe the difference that has been made in my life by knowing I have been sealed for eternity? What might I be doing to expand this difference?

6. Day Six: In baptism, I was *filled* with the Holy Spirit. By this filling I was …

- Adopted as God's child/born into God's family, the Church/made a living member of Christ's body, the church

Question: In what ways does knowing I have been adopted into God's family make a difference in my life? What personal rituals do I practice (or will I develop) to celebrate these differences?

CHAPTER 3

The Holy Spirit as the Power of God in the Liturgies for Holy Communion

The prayer book liturgies of both Baptism and Eucharist
make clear that it is not in the strength of the
signs – water, bread, and wine – that God is present,
but rather that the Spirit of God takes the signs
and makes them holy and powerful.
—James E. Griffiss, *The Anglican Vision*

As we begin our examination of Holy Communion, keep in mind
at least these three important beliefs about the Holy Spirit covered
in the two previous chapters.

- First, the phrase *the power of the Holy Spirit* is used in
  The American Book of Common Prayer and in the New
  Testament widely enough that it seems safe to affirm that,
  in *The American Book of Common Prayer*, the Holy Spirit
  is considered the *power* of God at work to make things
  happen "in the Church and in the world."
- Second, by action of the Holy Spirit, the water of baptism
  becomes a "sure and certain means by which we receive"
  the grace of God (according to our Catechism, BCP,
  p. 857).

- And third, the grace conveyed in Holy baptism carries with it a multitude of spiritual blessings (listed in summary at the end of Chapter 2 above).

In this chapter, we will notice three similar things relating the Holy Spirit to Holy Communion:

- First, the power of the Holy Spirit is invoked in the liturgies of Holy Communion to make something happen;
- Second, by action of the Holy Spirit, the Holy Communion elements of bread and wine become "sure and certain means by which we receive" the grace of God (according to our Catechism, BCP, p. 857);
- And third, the grace conveyed in Holy Communion carries with it a multitude of spiritual blessings.

The Holy Spirit Is Invoked to Sanctify the Bread and Wine of Holy Communion

There are eight prayers in *The American Book of Common Prayer* available to be used for consecrating the elements of Holy Communion. In all eight of these prayers, we are going to find two critical elements:

- We will find what are normally referred to as the words of institution (i.e., the words of Jesus, "This is my Body/ This is my Blood");
- And, we will also find an invocation of the Holy Spirit to sanctify the elements of bread and wine (the fancy word for this invocation is *epiclesis*"[23]).

---

[23] Epiclesis (or Epiklesis) is a Greek word meaning "to invoke" or to "call down upon."

Of the epiclesis, Griffiss says, "The same spirit [as that which sanctified the water of baptism] sanctifies the bread and wine of the Eucharist in order that they may be for us the Body and Blood of Jesus Christ" (Griffiss, op. cit., p. 118).

The presence of *both* the words of institution and the invocation of the Holy Spirit (epiclesis) in all eight prayers of consecration in *The American Book of Common Prayer* seems to indicate a belief that both are necessary; but, as we shall soon discover, the order in which they occur appears to be of lesser importance. (It is worth noting that in both the Roman Catholic and the Orthodox Churches, the words of institution and an epiclesis are also found.)

We will now examine the wording found in each of the eight canonical prayers for consecration, beginning with Rite I, the traditional liturgy most closely resembling the one found in *The 1928 American Book of Common Prayer.*

Rite I

In Rite I, the wording (following the wording of the 1928 liturgy) is as follows:

> ... of thy almighty goodness, vouchsafe to bless and sanctify, with thy Word and Holy Spirit, these gifts and creatures of bread and wine; that we, receiving them ... may be partakers of his most blessed Body and Blood (BCP, p. 335, line 19).

You may recall the definition of the word *sanctify* offered on the first page of Chapter 2. Sanctify can mean either to "set aside for God's work" or to "make Holy." We see here that two words are used: *bless*, which usually means to "set aside for God's work" *and sanctify.* So, in a sense, the Rite I liturgy, by using both bless and sanctify, is covering both bases. The bread and wine are being set aside for God's use and are being made holy as conveyances of God's manifold grace.

Also, in both alternative prayers of consecration for Rite I (pp. 333 and 340), "the Word" and "the Holy Spirit" are both mentioned. A logical assumption would seem to be that the Word refers to the words of institution and the Holy Spirit to the epiclesis, previously mentioned.

- This is a little confusing because usually when *Word* is capitalized in the New Testament and in the Prayer Book, it is referring to the person of Jesus, the *Logos* (Word) of God. (See, for example, John 1:1 and in the Prayer Book, the Collect for the Second Sunday in Lent, p. 166.) Here, however, it seems to make more sense to understand Word to mean the "words used by Jesus," i.e., the words of institution ("This is my Body ... my Blood") which define the grace to be received (i.e., the words identify the benefit to be received as partaking of "the Body and Blood of Christ").
- The Holy Spirit's role is to be the power by which the bread and wine are made into what Jesus says they are: his body and blood.

Rite II

In Rite II, Eucharistic Prayer A, the entire formula is simplified to:

> We offer you these gifts ... Sanctify them by your
> Holy Spirit to be for your people the Body and Blood
> of your Son (BCP, p. 363).

It should be mentioned that, even though the word *power* does not occur in any of the four forms of the prayer of consecration in Rite II, it would seem to make no sense to invoke the Holy Spirit if the words of institution were believed to be sufficient by themselves, or more specifically, were by themselves believed to contain the power by which the sanctifying of the bread and wine is made to happen. This seems to be consistent with New Testament teaching. In John's gospel, Jesus, speaking of the relationship between himself and the Holy Spirit, says, "He will glorify me, for he will take what is mine and declare it to you" (John 16:14).

In Rite II, Eucharistic Prayer B (BCP, p. 369), the petition is to:

> ... send your Holy Spirit upon these gifts that they may
> be the Sacrament (i.e., the means by which we receive) of
> the Body of Christ and his Blood of the new Covenant.

In Rite II, Eucharistic Prayer D (BCP, p. 375), the wording is:

> We pray that ... your Holy Spirit may descend
> upon ... these gifts, sanctifying them and showing
> them to be holy gifts for your holy people, the bread
> of life and the cup of salvation, the Body and Blood
> of your Son Jesus Christ.

In the section of the Prayer Book titled Communion under Special Circumstances" (BCP, p. 396f.), there are two forms of prayer for consecrating the elements of Holy Communion. The rubrical[24] directions specify that these forms are "intended for

---

[24] Rubrics are the small words of direction, sometimes thought of as the rules governing the usages in the Prayer Book. The word *rubric* comes from the Latin word for red because, in early versions of the BCP, the rubrics were actually printed in red.

use with those who for reasonable cause cannot be present at a public Celebration of the Eucharist." In other words, they may not be used on a Sunday or other congregational celebrations of Holy Communion.

Form two follows the pattern adhered to in Rite I and the three canonical prayers in Rite II mentioned above (A, B, and D), with the epiclesis coming *after* the words of institution. In this prayer, God the Father is asked:

> "Send your Holy Spirit upon these gifts. Let them be
> for us the Body and Blood of your Son." (BCP, p. 405)

Pertaining to the role of the Holy Spirit, Form 1 has the invocation of the Holy Spirit (epiclesis) *preceding* Jesus' words of institution; it nonetheless uses words closest to those found in Rite II, Prayer A:

> And so Father, we bring you these gifts. Sanctify them
> by your Holy Spirit to be for your people the Body and
> Blood of Jesus Christ our Lord (BCP, p. 403).

The only prayer of consecration contained in the Rite II liturgy that has the epiclesis coming *before* the words of institution is Eucharistic Prayer C (BCP, p. 371). The wording, after a lengthier introduction, follows closely that of Rite II, Prayer A, in asking:

> And so, Father, we who have been redeemed by him
> and made a new people by water and the Spirit, now
> bring before you these gifts. Sanctify them by your
> Holy Spirit to be the Body and Blood of Jesus Christ
> our Lord (BCP, p. 371).

So, while there are some slight differences of wording between the various options for the Eucharistic Prayers in both Rite I and II, and in the two Forms for Communion under Special Circumstances, the general meaning does not seem significantly altered. In all of them:

- the words of institution appear;
- the Holy Spirit is invoked as the power to make something happen;
- the *something* expected to happen always involves a change by virtue of which the bread and wine become a means through which the body and blood of Jesus is conveyed and received.

+ + The Benefits Conveyed in and through Holy Communion + +

Remember that the Catechism in *The Book of Common Prayer* defines sacraments as "outward and visible signs of" *and* "sure and certain *means* by which" we believers receive an "inward and spiritual grace." The graces or benefits received in baptism are summarized at the end of Chapter 2 above. What, then, are the "inward and spiritual graces" or benefits we can and should expect to receive through Holy Communion?

Our Catechism (BCP, pp. 859–860) mentions seven specific spiritual benefits:

1. The Catechism identifies one purpose for receiving the body and blood of Christ as being "for the continual remembrance of his life, death and resurrection until his coming again."

2. Next, we are told that Holy Communion is "the way by which the sacrifice of Christ is made present," and

3. It is the way "in which he unites us to his one offering of himself."

4. Last, in answer to the specific question, "What are the benefits which we receive in the Lord's Supper?" the Catechism mentions four specific benefits:

5. "we receive ... the forgiveness of our sins"

6. "the strengthening of our union with Christ"

7. "the strengthening of our union with one another"

8. And, "the foretaste of the heavenly banquet which is our nourishment in eternal life."

Assuming that our participation in Holy Communion is *purposeful,* that is, we participate in order to receive the benefits we are told to expect to receive, we should be able to agree that it is worth taking a few minutes to look at each of these graces or benefits individually.

First, the Catechism identifies one purpose for receiving the body and blood of Christ as being "for the continual remembrance of his life, death and resurrection until his coming again." The simplest form of this continual remembrance is contained at the end of each section of the words of institution. Jesus says, "This is my Body ... take and eat"/"This is my Blood ... drink it ... do this in remembrance of me." But the idea of Holy Communion as a remembrance [memorial] occurs in other places as well:

    o In the Collect for Maundy Thursday (BCP, p. 221), we are reminded that it was on this night that Jesus instituted this sacrament; we ask then to be granted the ability to "receive it thankfully in remembrance of Jesus Christ our Lord."

o In line three of the Exhortation (BCP, p. 316), we are again reminded of Maundy Thursday as the night in which Jesus instituted the sacrament "for the continual remembrance of the sacrifice of his death."

o Four times in Rite I, Eucharistic Prayer I (BCP, p. 335) and, similarly, in all seven of the other prayers of consecration (pp. 342, 362, 368, 371, 374, 403, 405), the phrase occurs to "Do this in remembrance."

It seems logical to want to know *why*? Why is it considered important for us to remember Christ's death? I want to mention three reasons for your consideration:

- As the Exhortation (BCP, p. 316) and some of the prayers of consecration suggest, to remember Christ's sacrificial death is to make ourselves mindful of the extent of God's great love for us;

- As we noted earlier, the Collect for Maundy Thursday (BCP, pp.221, 274) suggests that remembering engenders "thankfulness";

- Interpreters seem to disagree on the exact meaning of the word *anamnesis,* usually translated as "remembrance." It is possible to see *anamnesis* as meaning more than a mere mental consideration, but an actual participation through reenactment or re-actualization in the last meal Jesus shared with his disciples. Dom Gregory Dix, in his 1945 publication, *The Shape of the Liturgy,* supports this view.[25] In 1 Corinthians Paul talks about consumption of food previously offered as part of a sacrifice to pagan idols, comparing it with a Christian's consumption of the bread and the wine of Holy Communion. In 1 Corinthians 10:16 and context, Paul asks, "The cup of blessing which we bless, is it not a participation in the blood of Christ? The bread we break, is it not a participation in the body of Christ?" The Greek word translated *participation* in this verse is the word *koinonia* [κοιννία]. While the word has a variety of translations in its many uses in the New Testament, the most prominent meaning points to the sense of community or oneness that exists (or should exist) between Christians. Taking that as a starting place, it seems to me to make most sense to translate Paul's sentence in 1 Corinthians 10:16 in this way: "The cup of blessing which we bless, is it not a means of becoming one with the Blood of Christ? The bread we break, is it not a means of becoming one with the Body of Christ." This translation seems to be closest to the literal translation of the word *koinonia and* to the concept of *anamnesis* as a re-actualization of the event which took place on what we call Maundy Thursday.

Second, the Catechism tells us that Holy Communion is "the way by which the sacrifice of Christ is made present." (BCP, p. 859) Like many other theological issues in Anglicanism, there are varied interpretations of what this means. Evangelicals tend to reject the notion that Christ is *re-sacrificed* each time the Eucharist is celebrated; those who hold to a belief that Christ is re-sacrificed base their belief largely on a single verse

---

[25] From http://www.global.org/Pub/Shape_of_the_Liturgy.asp, Chapter 9, "The Meaning of the Eucharist," 238.

of Scripture found in Colossians 1:24.[26] In fact, when *The 1979 American Book of Common Prayer* was first introduced for trial use, many evangelical Episcopalians petitioned for the phrase, "Christ our Passover is sacrificed for us" (BCP, p. 337 and elsewhere) to read instead, "Christ our Passover WAS sacrificed for us." [emphasis added]

Many Episcopal believers seem to lump the idea of "making present Christ's sacrifice" with the previously mentioned notion of remembrance, that is, that in Holy Communion we are reminded in a powerful and vivid way of the sacrifice Christ made on our behalf. This point of view is voiced in Communion under Special Circumstances, Form 1 (BCP, p. 403):

> Father … By means of this holy bread and cup, we show forth the sacrifice of his death … until he comes again." Also in the proper preface for Easter (BCP, pp. 346, 379) we are told, "He is the very Paschal Lamb, who was sacrificed for us." In short, then, however it is interpreted or understood, we are offered in Holy Communion "the way by which the sacrifice of Christ is made present to and for us.

---

[26] Matthew Henry, a renowned eighteenth century evangelical expositor, explains Colossians 1:24 in these words: "Both the sufferings of the Head and of the members are called the sufferings of Christ, and make up, as it were, one body of sufferings. But He suffered for the redemption of the church; we suffer on other accounts; for we do but slightly taste that cup of afflictions of which Christ first drank deeply. A Christian may be said to fill up that which remains of the sufferings of Christ, when he takes up his cross, and after the pattern of Christ, bears patiently the afflictions God allots to him." Source: *Matthew Henry's Concise Commentary on the Bible.*

Third, Holy Communion is the way "in which he unites us to his one offering of himself." (BCP, p. 859) The implicit question is, in what way do we consider ourselves united with Christ's once and for all self-offering? To be sure, we are the recipients of the benefits of his self-offering, which are, namely, the forgiveness of our sins and salvation itself—both of which we lay claim to only by virtue of his self-offering. (See BCP, p. 369, "Unite us to your Son in his sacrifice, that we may be acceptable through him.") It would seem that the implication may be not so much that we are united with his sacrifice, but that, as we receive the body and blood of Christ by faith, we are reassured of receiving the benefits of his sacrifice.

Fourth, in Holy Communion we receive the forgiveness of our sins. These same words were used in the sacrament of holy baptism. So, it might seem logical here to ask, at what point in time do we receive forgiveness for our sins?

- Was it when Jesus died on the cross? (see Romans 5:6–9).
- Or was it at our baptism? (see Catechism, answer to question three in the section on holy baptism, BCP, p. 858).
- Or was it in the Service of Holy Communion (or Morning or Evening Prayer) when the priest pronounces us absolved, following our Confession?
- Or, as the Catechism seems to be suggesting, is it at the moment we consume the bread and wine of Holy Communion that our sins are forgiven? (BCP, p. 859)

In a certain sense, all four answers are correct. It seems though, doesn't it, as it is with so many other things in life, something doesn't become fully real until words become *action*. The Promises of Scripture, of baptism, of confession and absolution become experienced when we actually, physically become "one body with him, and he with us." (BCP, p. 336) The Collect of the Holy Eucharist" (BCP, p. 252) asks, "God our Father ... Grant us so to venerate the sacred mysteries of his Body and Blood that we may ever perceive within ourselves the fruit of his redemption." That is when forgiveness becomes real, isn't it? When we perceive within ourselves that he has embraced us totally and without reservation or qualification. This truth may be most clearly stated in the postcommunion prayer contained within the office for Ministration to the Sick, which affirms, "Gracious Father, we give you praise and thanks for this Holy Communion ... and we pray that it may bring us forgiveness of our sins ..." (BCP p. 457).

Fifth, in Holy Communion we are told that we experience "the strengthening of our union with Christ." (BCP, p. 860) This seems to be yet another way in which the connection between baptism and Holy Communion re-emerges. Our Catechism (Holy Baptism, p. 858) tells us that "The inward and spiritual grace in Baptism is union with Christ ..." And then, in the catechetical section on Holy Communion, we are told that one of the benefits of Holy Communion is "the strengthening of our union with Christ" (BCP, p. 860).

I remember passing one of those Churches with a sign board in front containing the quotation: "If you don't feel close to God ... Who moved?" The truth is, we sin, we drift, and we fail to live up to the promises made in baptism and reaffirmed in confirmation. Our union with Christ needs the reaffirmation, renewal, and re-strengthening we find through Holy Communion because, while *he* may remain constant, *we* move. It is powerfully reassuring to be reminded that we, being "partakers of ... Holy Communion, may be ... made one body with him, that he may dwell in us and we in him." As the Collect for the Fourth Sunday in Lent pleads, "Evermore give us this bread, that he may live in us and we in him" (BCP, p. 219).

Sixth, another benefit of Holy Communion is "the strengthening of our union with one another." (BCP, p. 860) The passing of the peace, the common cup, the *we* wording of the Nicene Creed and the prayers all serve to remind us that we gather at the holy table as a living and inter-connected organism, the body of Christ.

I remember one church I served where we followed a fairly common practice of having an early Rite I Service and a later Rite II Service. Typically, the early service was participated in by a smaller number of people than the later service. What troubled me was not the small number of people at the eight o'clock service, but the fact that the fifteen people would sit (it seemed conscious and intentional) as far apart from one another as they possibly could. It was like their personal theology (such as it was) was just for each individual and God; the other people present, while tolerated, did not seem for them to be necessary for their worship to be full and meaningful. It often seems so hard to get the message across: we are a *we*. We are the body of Christ corporately. And our corporate-ness *is* necessary. While I specifically want to talk in Chapter 4 about the role of the Holy Spirit in helping create and maintain a stronger sense of *we-ness*, I will mention here just a few places in the Prayer Book where Holy Communion is described as serving to "strengthen our union with one another."

- Toward the end of Eucharistic Prayer C (BCP, p. 372), we pray: "Let the grace of this Holy Communion make us one body, one spirit in Christ."

- And in Prayer D, we ask: "Grant that all who share this bread and cup, may become one body and one spirit, a living sacrifice in Christ ..." (BCP, p. 375).

Both of these Prayer Book references seem to express a theology consistent with what is called the "High Priestly Prayer" of Jesus that occupies the totality of John, chapter 17. In this prayer Jesus prays: "Father, make them one as you and I are one, so the world will know that you sent me."

Seventh, we are told that Holy Communion is "the foretaste of the heavenly banquet which is our nourishment in eternal life." (Catechism, p. 860). It is somewhat confusing to me that the only two liturgical references using this phrase are in our Burial Offices, both occurrences found in the postcommunion prayers used in place of the customary postcommunion prayer of thanksgiving (see BCP, pp. 482, 498). While it is true that burial is a specific time we look for special reassurance of the connection between this life and the next, I find it lacking that the connection is not made more strongly in every Eucharistic celebration. If we are *trained* to see it, the connection is certainly present every time we repeat:

Therefore we praise you, joining our voices with Angels and Archangels and with all the company of heaven, who forever sing this hymn to proclaim the glory of your name: Holy, Holy, Holy, etc.

In 1967 I had the pleasure of hearing a well-known theologian speak. He had just a few years earlier started teaching at a distinguished seminary in New York City and had been ordained an Episcopal priest in 1965. In his talk he explained why he was opposed to moving altars away from the wall of the church to the freestanding placement where we find most Episcopal altars today.

He suggested that, at the point in the liturgy where we proclaim the joining of our voices with angels and archangels and the entire company of heavenly occupants, we ought to use our imaginations to envision the back wall (behind the altar) of the church momentarily falling away, giving us a brief realization that what we see as the altar is really the end of a long table extending all the way into heaven. Jesus is seated at the head of the table with the apostles and all the saints in heaven, occupying seats down both sides of the table, stretching all the way into our nave and catching us up for this one moment in time into the host of heavenly beings and voices. This allows us to join with them in their unending hymn of "Holy, Holy, Holy." Now, to me, *that* is truly what one of the benefits of Holy Communion means— to experience a "foretaste of the heavenly banquet which is our nourishment in eternal life."

Questions for Further Thought or Discussion

1. Most Protestant denominations offer Scripture readings, a sermon, prayers, and sacred music as a usual worship experience; in these traditions, Holy Communion, if offered at all on a Sunday, occurs about four times per year. While there are exceptions, the norm in Episcopal churches is to offer Holy Communion as "the principal act of worship."

   Question: Would you miss Holy Communion if it were not offered weekly? Put into words why you would miss it.

2. The Roman Catholic theological doctrine concerning Holy Communion is called *transubstantiation,* which means to "change substance." This belief holds that the substance of the bread and wine actually changes to a different substance, namely the body and blood of Christ. While Lutherans themselves do not employ the term, Catholics refer to the Lutheran doctrine concerning Holy Communion as *consubstantiation* to distinguish it from their own belief. Loosely translated, consubstantiation means that the bread and wine do not become the body and blood of Christ, but rather, they coexist alongside one another. In typical Episcopal fashion, we don't take one side or the other, but simply affirm that the real presence of Christ is manifested to believers by means of the bread and the wine of Holy Communion.

   Question: Does one view seem to have more appeal to you than the others? Put into words why it does or does not?

3. Much has been said in this book so far about the power of the Holy Spirit.

   Question: Given your understanding of Holy Communion, what difference does it make to you personally that this power is invoked (invited in, as it were) into the celebration of Holy Communion? Do you believe anything is really different because of the invocation of the Holy Spirit? Describe what and how?

4. It is normal for a communicant to bring some expectations when coming to worship and receive Holy Communion? Make a list of experiences you have had personally that convince you that your expectations are or have been met?

Using the following scale, indicate the frequency with which the above mentioned conscious expectations are normally met:

(5)　Always

(4)　Almost Always

(3)　Almost Never

(2)　Never

(1)　I've never thought about it before.

Reflect briefly on your answer.

Question: Are you satisfied or dissatisfied with your answer? What action do you feel motivated to take as a result of what your answer reveals to you?

5. Think back over the graces you received in baptism (at the end of Chapter 2 above). Describe (a) what effect regularly receiving Holy Communion should have on the development of those graces in your life. (b) What evidence do you see in your life that regularly receiving Holy Communion actually *is* having a visible effect on the development of baptismal graces in your life?

6. Question: What action do you feel motivated to take as a result of what your answer reveals to you?

7. Think back over the graces or benefits that are intended to be conveyed and received through participating in Holy Communion.

　　a)　The Catechism identifies one purpose for receiving the body and blood of Christ "as being "for the continual remembrance of his life, death and resurrection until his coming again";

b)   Next, we are told, Holy Communion is "the way by which the sacrifice of Christ is made present;" and

c)   It is the way "in which he unites us to his one offering of himself."

d)   Last, in answer to the specific question, "What are the benefits which we receive in the Lord's supper?" the Catechism mentions four specific benefits:

- "we receive … the forgiveness of our sins"
- "the strengthening of our union with Christ"
- "the strengthening of our union with one another" and
- "the foretaste of the heavenly banquet which is our nourishment in eternal life."

Question: To what extent are you usually aware of these benefits as you approach to receive Holy Communion? Do you feel more motivated to take some action that might make you more conscious of these benefits? If so, what?

CHAPTER 4

The Holy Spirit as the Power of God in Believers' Lives

I remarked in Chapter1 that the Holy Spirit is the power of God in and with us ordinary believers. We are filled with the Holy Spirit in baptism. And, by the power of the Holy Spirit invoked in Holy Communion, the bread and wine are made "sure and certain means by which we receive" the grace of God, namely, being united with Christ and his sacrifice. The logical question would seem to be, "So, isn't that enough?" Isn't it sufficient for me to have been baptized, to confirm my faith before a bishop and to receive Holy Communion regularly so that I am forgiven and re-united with Christ? My answer (and I believe the answer given all of us Episcopalians in our Prayer Book) is no! It isn't. The reason is that there is much in us that needs changing, and it will take more than a lifetime to accomplish it. Being all that God wants us to be is a lifelong undertaking. He gives us all the tools we need, but it is up to us to cooperate with God's program of change.

What I have just said might seem confusing at first. Some readers may be wondering, if the graces conveyed in baptism were presented as being permanent gifts (or graces)—for example, that in our baptism, we are "cleansed from sin ... made able to continue in the risen life of Christ ... and provided all things necessary to be sustained in our Christian life" (see complete list at the end of Chapter 2 above)—why do we need to continue to ask for forgiveness, and why do we need to pray daily for renewal? These are good questions for which many saints and theologians have suggested answers. Here is the answer that makes most sense to me.

When you and I are baptized, God sees us as perfect and *re-names* us as *perfect*. Paul, in his writings (especially in Romans 4:5-6), uses the language of financial accounting in saying that God "credits perfection (i.e., righteousness) to our account." In other words, from the moment of my baptism, to God I am *perfect John*. That's the way he thinks of me and the way he refers to me. But, is it the way that I really am? Do I suddenly begin to act perfectly in every situation? Do I suddenly act and think morally pure actions and thoughts every moment of every day? Obviously not. The perfection which God has credited to us—the perfect image of Christ, which is the measure of the perfection God wants us to attain[27]—needs to be worked out in detail in the reality of our lives.

To further complicate this process of working out the details of our perfection, there are many forces working against us. Our human ego, temptations of the flesh, and (depending on how you think of Satan[28]) external forces of evil seek to lure us onto a path that does not lead to our perfect self. For some people, parts of the Prayer Book sound old fashioned. Yet, since the old-fashioned sounding words express timeless truths, they still have relevance for us if we are willing to hear them. The Great Litany, for example, petitions, "From all inordinate and sinful affections, and from the deceits of the world, the flesh and the devil ... Good Lord, deliver us." (BCP, p. 48f.) All of these forces are working

---

[27] See 2 Corinthians 3:18 and Ephesians 4:13.

[28] See Ephesians 6:10–17.

against us in our effort to work out the perfection accounted to us by God.

A look at just a few references in the Prayer Book would seem to confirm this interpretation of the objective of the Christian life.

- Our Catechism tells us that "The Holy Spirit is revealed as the Lord who leads us into all truth and enables us to grow in the likeness of Christ" (BCP p. 852).
- As a bishop lays hands on a confirmand he or she says, "Defend, O Lord, your servant N. with your heavenly grace that *he* may ... daily increase in your Spirit more and more" (BCP, p. 418).
- In the Collect of a Pastor, we pray that, "following [our pastor's] example and teaching ... we may by your grace grow into the stature of the fullness of our Lord and Savior Jesus Christ" (BCP, p. 248).

If you are willing to accept this explanation, then it should be easier to see that the working out of the perfection in which we are already seen by God becomes a lifelong purpose, desired by God and made possible by God's very own power examined in Chapter 1—namely, the Holy Spirit we received at baptism.

Here I believe is the exciting challenge available to every Episcopalian. Maybe your parents weren't told it when they presented you for baptism. Maybe you didn't have it properly explained when you were preparing for confirmation. Maybe it hasn't been said clearly in the sermons and Sunday school classes you have attended. But here it is now.

Are you willing to accept this as your life purpose and objective?

To grow daily more and more into the full stature
of Christ, within the body of Christ, and to serve as

a member of his royal priesthood, strengthened and
supported by the power of God's Holy Spirit.

The main reason I have chosen to base this study on *The American Book of Common Prayer,* rather than on another authoritative source such as the Bible, is that I believe many Episcopalians seem to believe that people have so twisted the Bible to mean what they want it to mean that no single interpretation can be trusted. My hope here is that by mainly using references from our Prayer Book, I will convince at least some readers that the purpose stated above really is what God wants all of us to be working toward. We may have not seen it in the past, but here it is. And if we choose to accept it and adopt it as our own personal statement of life purpose, then we will move ahead together to discover how to cooperate with God's Spirit in living into this purpose.

The Holy Spirit, which we all received at baptism, is pursuing five objectives in our lives:

1. To *transform* us. Paul, writing in Ephesians, chapter 4, uses the phrase, "until all of us come to ... maturity, measured by nothing less than the full stature of Christ" (v. 13).

2. To *support* us. The general idea surrounding this work of the Holy Spirit in our lives is that when we are feeling discouraged or hopeless, the Spirit is with us to provide encouragement and reassurance. In John 14:26, for example, Jesus refers to the Comforter (other translations use advocate, counselor); the Greek word is *paraclete,* meaning "the one who is called to be beside you."

3. To *strengthen* us. The Holy Spirit is the present source of empowerment for our service in Christ's kingdom. (See in the Liturgy for Confirmation, BCP, p. 419, line 10.)

4. To *draw us close* to God. In the Prayer for Quiet Confidence, we ask, "By the might of your Spirit lift us, we pray, into your presence, where we may be still and know that you are God" (BCP, p. 832, #59).

5. To *unify* us with other Christians. In the Prayer for the Unity of the Church, we pray to "be united in one body by the one Spirit" (BCP, p. 255, #14).

Let's now look at each of these five objectives individually as they are defined and described in our Prayer Book.

Part I: The Holy Spirit Wants to Work in Us to Transform Us.

The references to our postbaptismal transformation fall into three general areas:

(a) the **goal** of transformation, namely sanctification and holiness;

(b) the **prerequisite** of transformation, surrendering control

(c) the **method** of transformation, being led into all truth

(A) The Goal of Transformation

The section of Collects for Various Occasions, number seven, "For All Baptized Christians," verbalizes the connection between what has already been received in baptism and what still has to be worked out. It asks God to:

"Grant ... to all who have been baptized into the death and resurrection of your Son Jesus Christ, that, as we have put away the old life of sin, so we may be renewed in the spirit of our minds and live in righteousness and true holiness." (BCP, pp. 252–253).

This process of transforming our lives so that we are moving toward the actual perfection ("righteousness and true holiness"), which God already credited to our account, goes by many theological terms in our Prayer Book: sanctification, amendment of life, being made holy, and renewing us; they are all terms used in *The American Book of Common Prayer*. Here I will include one clear example of a place that each of these words or phrases occurs, and then other examples will be listed in Appendix D for those who might like to take a more extensive look.

Sanctify

Included in Rite II, Eucharistic Prayers A, B, and D is some form of the request for sanctification. In Prayer A, immediately following the epiclesis (see Appendix C), the priest continues, "And sanctify us also that we may faithfully receive this holy sacrament" (BCP, p. 363).

Amend Our Lives

The Prayers of the People, Form V includes the petition, "For ourselves, for the forgiveness of our sins, and for the grace of the Holy Spirit to amend our lives, we pray to you, O Lord" (BCP, p. 391).

Make Us Holy

When a bishop blesses the altar during the consecration of a church, he or she says in one petition of the prayers: "We praise you for sending your Holy Spirit to make us holy, etc." (BCP, p. 573).

Renewal

A collect which may be used at confirmation in place of the Collect of the Day asks: "Grant, Almighty God, that we, who have been redeemed from the old life of sin by our baptism into the death and resurrection of your Son Jesus Christ, may be renewed in your Holy Spirit and live in righteousness and true holiness" (BCP, p. 254).

(B) Surrendering Control in Order to Be Transformed

Ruler and Governor

Most readers will be aware of the multiple references in the Old Testament to God as *King*. Psalm 99 says: "The Lord reigns ... he is enthroned upon cherubim." Likewise, in the New Testament, Jesus makes numerous references to God's kingdom. Most Bible linguists seem to agree that the Greek word normally translated *kingdom*, *basilea (Basileia)*, would be more accurately translated *kingship*, referring to the sway or influence of the king. In Matthew 6:33 Jesus tells us to "Seek first the *basilea* of God and His righteousness." It should not surprise us, then, to discover numerous references in our Prayer Book to God's governance in our lives.

In An Order of Service for Noonday, a collect asks God to "send your Holy Spirit into our hearts, to direct and rule us according to your will" (BCP, p. 107). The collect "for all Christians in their vocation" is prayed to "Almighty and everlasting God, by whose Spirit the whole body of your faithful people is governed" (BCP, pp. 206, 256). Many Episcopal congregations, on the last Sunday after Pentecost, celebrate Christ the King Sunday, at which time we may use a collect for the "The Reign of Christ" (BCP, p. 254).

While we may acknowledge the presence of these references and admit to using the prayers referred to above, it is admittedly difficult for many modern Americans especially to internalize the spiritual concept of being ruled and governed by God. First of all, we rejected kingly rule as a nation in 1776; but more recently, the idea of doing your own thing has pervaded our culture. One of the most celebrated essays in American literature is *Self Reliance* by Ralph Waldo Emerson. In it he extols the virtue of relying on one's own perception and discernment. Clearly, the idea of being ruled and governed by God is one of the more challenging ideas presented us in our faith, as practiced using the prayers and liturgies of *The American Book of Common Prayer*.

(C) The Method of Transformation—
Being Led into All Truth

Guidance

Morning Prayer I and II include "A Collect for Guidance" (BCP, pp. 57 and 100), in which "We humbly pray thee so to guide and govern us by thy Holy Spirit, that in all the cares and occupations of our life we may … remember that we are ever walking in thy sight."

While many of the prayers and collects assembled in *The American Book of Common Prayer* are for us as individuals, some are written for the church as a whole, such as the prayer "For the choice of fit persons for the ministry" (BCP, number II on pp. 205, 256). The petition in this prayer is for God to "Grant that your Church, under the guidance of your Holy Spirit, may choose suitable persons for the ministry of Word and Sacrament."

Direction

Though it may only be a nuance of difference, guiding seems to indicate a more personal, hands-on type of leadership, possibly even accompanying a person on their quest (as a field guide). This seems to fit with the idea of the Holy Spirit as Paraclete, set forth in the section entitled Comfort (below, p. 90), as a spiritual guide who *comes alongside of* us. The word *direct* seems to imply more of an administrative, down-from-above sort of routing. One definition of the word *direct* offered in *Webster's Dictionary* is "to enjoin with authority." It is little wonder, then, that the word *direct* is most often coupled with the word *rule* when used in *The American Book of Common Prayer*. For example, in both traditional and contemporary language versions, the Collect for Proper 19 asks: "Grant that your Holy Spirit may in all things direct and rule our hearts" (BCP, pp. 182, 233).

Leads into All Truth

In John's gospel Jesus further describes the Holy Spirit as "the Spirit of truth" (John 15:26 and 16:13) whose role it is to "teach you all things" (John 14:26) and to "guide you into all truth"

(John 16:13).[29] The Proper Preface for Pentecost in both Rite I and Rite II, which refers to the apostles as the original recipients of the Holy Spirit on Pentecost, uses the phrase, "lead them into all truth" (BCP, pp. 347, 380), whereas the Proper Preface for Baptism says, "you have … given us the Holy Spirit to guide us into all truth." An Order of Service for Noonday, however, includes a collect asking, "Heavenly Father, send your Holy Spirit into our hearts … to lead us into all truth" (BCP, p. 107). I judge from this that the editors of *The American Book of Common Prayer* saw the words *guide* and *lead* as completely synonymous and used both without implying any difference.

Part II: The Holy Spirit Wants to Work in Us to Support Us

The prayer said by the bishop immediately following the act of baptism includes these words: "Heavenly Father, we thank you that by water and the Holy Spirit you have bestowed upon this your servant the forgiveness of sin, and have raised them to the new life of grace. Sustain them, O Lord, in your Holy Spirit." (BCP, p. 308) The implication here seems to be that God, by his Holy Spirit, will supply the necessary energy for each of us to live our postbaptismal life without worrying or feeling overwhelmed.

Sustain

Probably most familiar to many who regularly use the Daily Office is the occurrence of this phrase at the end of Suffrages A.

---

[29] Some translations say "lead you into all truth." The Greek word *hodegio* (odhgew) is translated as both guide and lead.

V. Create in us clean hearts, O God;

R. And sustain us with your Holy Spirit (BCP, p. 98).

Uphold

While somewhat vague, the meaning of the word *uphold* is clear in its linkage with amended life in the Prayer of Confession: "and so uphold us by your Spirit that we may live and serve you in newness of life" (BCP, p. 393; Prayers of the People, Form VI). While living in North Carolina we experienced a lot of "black ice", often hidden beneath a light dusting of snow. I remember during one of these times seeing a couple walking along the sidewalk with the husband's aging father supported on each side by the couple tightly grasping his arms. That became a kind of visual image of how the Spirit -- the *paraclete* – upholds us through challenging times and circumstances.

Comfort

The term used by Jesus in John's gospel to describe the Holy Spirit is the Greek term Paraclete (paraklhtos). In English, depending on the Bible translation, this word is most often translated counselor or Comforter. The term literally translated means *the one called alongside*, thus giving us an image of the Holy Spirit standing beside us, not only to uphold us, but to give comfort, support, strength, or encouragement. We often think of the term counselor or comforter as someone trying to restore peace or calm to someone who is agitated by tragedy or grief.

The word *comfort* literally means "with fortitude" and may more accurately be translated "strength giver." Interestingly, in the traditional language of the Collect for Easter 7, the prayer pleads, "leave us not comfortless, but send us thine Holy Ghost to comfort us." However, the contemporary language collect for the same Sunday says, "do not leave us comfortless, but send us your Holy Spirit to strengthen us," thus encompassing both implications of the word (BCP, Seventh Sunday of Easter, pp. 175, 226).

Console

I believe, while the difference may be slight, that there is a difference between comfort and consolation. In Matthew's version of the Beatitudes (Matthew 5:4) Jesus says "Blessed are those who mourn for they shall be comforted." If we truly mourn over our sinfulness, having our grief and guilt over our sin lifted seems more an act of consolation than of comfort. Three times, in Rite I Morning and Evening Prayer, and Rite I Penitential Office, the absolution following the confession states:

> "The Almighty and merciful Lord grant you absolution and remission of all your sins, true repentance, amendment of life and the grace and consolation of his Holy Spirit." (BCP, pp. 42, 63, 321).

Part III: The Holy Spirit Wants to Work in Us to Strengthen and Empower Us

Strengthen

In baptism we are made to share in the royal priesthood of Jesus Christ. The Collect for the Holy Spirit asks God to "grant that by the indwelling of your Holy Spirit we may be … strengthened for your service" (BCP, p. 251, number 2). How often do we seek to do God's work in our own strength when we have access to the empowerment of God's Spirit which would make the work we do in God's name so much more effective. This is reflected in one of the optional sentences a bishop may use in the liturgy for confirmation: "Strengthen, O lord, your servant N. with your Holy Spirit; empower him/her for your service, etc." (BCP, p. 418).

Part IV: The Holy Spirit Wants to Work in Us to Draw Us Close to God.

Closeness to God

Finally, even though we are "made an inheritor of the kingdom of God" and "born into God's family" in baptism, we continue to ask to be drawn closer to God by his Spirit, as in the Prayer for Quiet Confidence (BCP, p. 832, #59).

> "O GOD of peace, who hast taught us that in returning and rest we shall be saved, in quietness and in confidence shall be our strength; By the might of thy Spirit lift us, we pray thee, to thy presence, where we may be still and know that thou art God; through Jesus Christ our Lord. Amen."

One of the most common requests I hear when people seek me out for Spiritual Direction is "I want to feel closer to God." James 4:8 reminds us that God has the same desire – that we draw close to Him, for he wants to be as close to us as we do to Him.

Part V: The Holy Spirit Wants to Work in Us to Help Us to Be United with Other Christians

We are accustomed to many of our prayers and collects ending with a Trinitarian phrase like, "Through Jesus Christ our Lord, who lives and reigns with God the Father, in the unity of the Holy Spirit." Some form of the phrase, "in the unity of the Holy Spirit" occurs more than sixty times in *The American Book of Common Prayer.*

The doctrine of the Trinity, formulated in the early fourth century, basically states that one God exists in three persons having but one substance: the three persons are called Father, Son, and Holy Spirit; the one substance, it seems, is in the form of "Spirit." Thus the Holy Spirit, while one of the *persons* of the Godhead, is also the unifying power within the Trinity. While the Holy Spirit is not mentioned by Jesus in his high priestly prayer in John, chapter 17, Jesus does pray that members of his church will be one "as my heavenly Father and I are one" (John 17:22b). If "as" is interpreted to mean "in the same way," then we could infer that the unifying work of the Holy Spirit within the Trinity is the same power summoned by the church to establish and maintain unity among Christians.

This understanding of the unifying role of the Holy Spirit does in fact fit with Paul's understanding in Ephesians 4:3, where he refers to *unity* as "unity of the Spirit," saying, "strive to maintain the unity of the Spirit in the bond of peace."

In our Prayer Book, relational unity within the Church is requested using a number of fairly synonymous terms: bound, united, gathered, knit, and made one. In addition, the prayers fall into a small number of purposeful categories.

Mission

Possibly one of the most important categories is for church members to maintain their unity so that they can succeed in their mission.

Prayer for the Unity of the Church #14, referring to Jesus' prayer in John, chapter 17, says:

> "Almighty Father, whose blessed Son before his passion prayed for his disciples that they might be one, as you and he are one: Grant that your Church, being bound together in love and obedience to you, may be united in one body by the one Spirit, **that the world may believe in him whom you have sent**." (BCP, pp. 204, 255). [emphasis added]

And Proper 16 asks: "Grant … that your Church, being gathered together in unity by your Holy Spirit, may show forth your power among all peoples" (BCP, pp. 181, 232).

The church is called to be a living witness to the un-churched world that God's Spirit transforms people. The world should be streaming to our door wanting what we are supposed to have—a new way of living together. If we can succeed in finding the Spirit's way to this new life, we will no longer be a denomination in decline. Our constant and unrelenting prayer must be: "Spirit, empower us to live together in unity so that the world may believe in him whom you have sent."

Our transformation not only involves desiring, learning how, and working at being unified in the body of Christ, the church, it involves other evidences that the power of God changes lives. It is fitting and understandable that our prayers include calling out to the Spirit to make our actions holy and keep our love pure.

The bishop, in his prayer for blessing the altar in the consecration of a church, says, "We praise you for sending your Holy Spirit to make us holy, and to unite us in your holy Church" (BCP, p. 573).

The Collect for Proper 9 prays: "Grant us the grace of your Holy Spirit, that we may be ... united to one another with pure affection" (BCP, pp. 179, 230).

Firm Foundation

Jesus tells a wonderful parable about building a house on sand, versus building it on a solid stone foundation. In 1 Corinthians 3:11, Paul reminds us, "no other foundation can be laid than the one which has already been laid which is Jesus Christ." It is important to remember that if our efforts in mission, outreach, and service to others are built upon this solid spiritual and theological foundation, then our labors will be valuable and effective.

The Collect for Saints Peter and Paul asks: "Grant that Your Church, instructed by their teaching and example and knit together in unity by your Spirit, may ever stand firm upon the one foundation ..." (BCP, pp. 190, 241).

Supportive Fellowship

The author of the letter to the Hebrews comments on what we have traditionally referred to as "the communion of saints." This communion is made up of currently living Christians and those who have died and are now in heaven. The support of this communion of believers makes it possible for our efforts to be empowered beyond our human abilities as we go about doing the work of God's kingdom. The author says: "Therefore, since we are surrounded by so great a cloud of witnesses, let us also lay aside every weight and the sin that clings so closely, and let us run with perseverance the race that is set before us" (Hebrews 12:1).

A number of our prayers refer to this supportive communion. The general Collect of a Saint (option three) addresses God, saying: "by your Holy Spirit you have made us one with your saints in heaven and on earth: Grant that in our earthly pilgrimage we may always be supported by this fellowship of love and prayer" (BCP, pp. 199, 250, 395).

The concluding blessing in the service of Thanksgiving for a Child includes: "May God the Holy Spirit, who has made the Church one family, keep you in peace" (BCP, p. 445).

In Evening Prayer I and II, Suffrages B entreats: "That we may be bound together by thy Holy Spirit in the communion of ... all thy saints" (BCP, pp. 68, 122).

Collect for the Absent #52 entreats God "graciously to behold and bless those whom we love, now absent from us ... and grant that both they and we ... may be bound together by thy love in the communion of thy Holy Spirit" (BCP, p. 830).

Responsive Love

First John 4:19 says: "We love because God first loved us." The love of Christians toward one another and toward the outcast of the world is *responsive* love. Once we begin to grasp the full extent of God's unqualified love for us—his grace—the only appropriate response is to show love toward others as an act of gratitude.

A prayer for mission in both Evening Prayer I and II asks: "Send forth upon us the Spirit of love, that in companionship with one another your abounding grace may increase among us" (BCP, pp. 71, 125).

Like all the other prayers, collects, offices, and liturgical words that we Episcopalians speak when we are together, these prayers about the unifying work and harmonizing power of the Holy Spirit cry out to be more than words. Rather, they express the desire and intentions of our hearts. The Holy Spirit may be the energizing force that makes unity possible; but ours are the minds, hearts, bodies, and souls through whom this power chooses to work. Paul tells the Philippian Christians that he was glad to hear that they are "standing firm in one spirit, with one mind striving [Greek *agonizomai* literally means to agonize] side by side for the faith of the Gospel" (Philippians 1:27). What a beautiful picture of unity at work to be a supportive community to accomplish mission in the church. If this were to happen, I believe no Episcopal congregation would be struggling just to survive.

Summary

At the beginning of this chapter, I suggested one way of thinking about how what happens in baptism is connected with the ongoing work of the Holy Spirit in our lives. It included the following:

1. God credits to us the perfect image of Christ at our Baptism.
2. However, though God sees and thinks of us as perfect, actual perfection needs to be worked out in detail in the reality of our lives.
3. To further complicate this process of working out the details of our perfection, there are many forces working against us, such as our human ego, temptations of the flesh, and (depending on how you think of Satan) external forces of evil seeking to lure us onto a path that does not lead to our perfect self.

4. For some people, parts of the Prayer Book sound old-fashioned. Even though talk like this may seem either old-fashioned or even a little crazy or fanatical, it is language that expresses ideas that are instrumental to the theological world view presented us in our *American Book of Common Prayer.*

5. The power that propels us in our pursuit of transformation and is our ally in the battle against the "world, the flesh, and the devil" is God's very own power which we examined in Chapter 1, namely, the Holy Spirit we received at baptism. In the Catechism we read: "The Holy Spirit is revealed [in the new covenant] as the Lord who ... enables us to grow into the likeness of Christ" (BCP, p. 852).

6. The transformational work of the Holy Spirit in our lives has many aspects to it, including the goal to make us holy, also includes our need to surrender control to God and to look to the Holy Spirit to reveal Truth to us.

Questions for Further Thought or Discussion

1. Of the four words describing the transformational goal of the Holy Spirit following baptism (sanctify, amend, make holy, and renew (BCP, pp. 84–85),

    a. Which one are you most aware of? Describe what has made you aware of it.

    b. Which one do you find most difficult or challenging? Why?

    c. Where in your life is the work of transformation still needed the most? What is your plan to cooperate with this work of the Holy Spirit in you?

2. When you hear the idea of letting God rule and govern in your life, what do you find most challenging? In what ways have you experienced the greatest success in this area?

3. When you hear the idea of letting the Holy Spirit lead you into all truth, how have you experienced this happening? Is there anything you regularly do to allow the Spirit to lead you to truth?

4. Of the sections of this chapter on the supporting and sustaining work of the Spirit, how are you most aware of the Spirit doing this for you? What actions do you take to allow the Spirit to support and sustain you?

5. Of the sections of this chapter on the strengthening and empowering work of the Spirit, how are you most aware of this happening for you? What actions do you take to tap into the Spirit for strength and empowerment?

6. Think again about what is written in the section of this chapter on closeness to God.
    a. Are you satisfied with how close you feel to God? Why or why not?
    b. In what way(s) do you usually experience closeness with God?
    c. What is your plan for continuing or increasing your sense of closeness to God?

APPENDICES

APPENDIX A

The Holy Spirit as a Coequal Person of the Trinity

While it may seem self-evident to some readers that the Holy Spirit is a coequal person within the Godhead,[30] there may be others unfamiliar with the Christian understanding of God as a trinity of equal persons. So, I am including this Appendix to address this most basic concept of God's identity, namely, that God is three equal persons and that the Holy Spirit is one of these equal persons of God's character and identity.

Therefore, my objectives in this appendix are:

1. To show that Episcopal Christian worship, as we find it in the offices of *The American Book of Common Prayer* (1979), solidly holds to the orthodox belief in a triune God;
2. To give examples of how, throughout the BCP the Holy Spirit is included as a coequal member and person within the Trinitarian Godhead;
   - I will begin with examples of the simplest form of Trinitarian language in the prayer book that includes the Holy Spirit. This is often referred to as the Trinitarian formulary (i.e., "Father, Son, and Holy Spirit, one God").

---

[30] "Godhead" is a term often used to describe the totality of God as he reveals himself (see Colossians 2:9).

- I will also identify and discuss exceptions to this basic formulary as they occur in the BCP.

Trinitarian Episcopal Belief as Defined in the Catechism

In the Catechism (BCP, p. 852f.) in the 1979 revised BCP, the following three questions (with answers) appear:

Q. What then is the Athanasian Creed?
A. The Athanasian Creed is an ancient document proclaiming the nature of the Incarnation and of God as Trinity.

Q. What is the Trinity?
A. The Trinity is one God, Father, Son, and Holy Spirit.

Q. Who is the Holy Spirit?
A. The Holy Spirit is the third person of the Trinity, God at work in the world and in the church, even now.

Trinitarian Belief Defended from Holy Scripture

Trinitarian churches[31] have long been criticized by a few groups who make the accusation that the word *Trinity* is nowhere mentioned in Holy Scripture. While this is literally true, it has

---

[31] Nearly all major denominations of the Christian Church, Catholic, Orthodox, and Protestant profess doctrinal or creedal belief in the Trinity as defined in the Catechism.

been believed throughout Christian history by nearly all major Christian groups that there is sufficient evidence in Scripture to infer (conclude by deduction) that God exists as three persons. For example:

> In Genesis 1:26, God (the Creator, Father) uses a plural pronoun in saying, "Let us make humankind in our own image."

> Paralleling this thought, John begins his gospel (John 1:1–3) with reference to Jesus (whom John refers to as "the Word") as being present with the Creator-Father at the time of creation.

> Later in John's gospel (chapters 14:15f. and 16:4f), Jesus claims that he (Jesus) will be the one who sends the Holy Spirit to believers.

> Paul unhesitatingly refers to the Holy Spirit as a coequal partner in the Trinity. In 1 Corinthians 2:1–16 Paul states the claim that by having the indwelling Holy Spirit, a believer actually has the very "mind of Christ" himself.

> In Romans 8:5–11 Paul says that "anyone who does not have the Spirit" (whom Paul here calls "the Spirit of Christ"), "does not belong to him" (that is, to Christ).

Hopefully, these passages of Scripture provide sufficient proof that orthodox Christian churches do have a biblical basis for believe in a Trinitarian God (i.e., a God made up of three coequal persons, of which one is the Holy Spirit).

Next, I want to show how this belief in a Trinitarian God is also the belief of the Episcopal Church, expressed in the language of its worship.

The Collects and Prayers

In *The Book of Common Prayer*, prayers typically end with some form of the Trinitarian formulary (meaning a fixed form or formula-like). The most common, probably, is the phrase, "[Through] Jesus Christ [our Lord], who lives and reigns with you and the Holy Spirit, one God ..." [32]

However, there are numerous variations of this formula. For example at the end of the Collects for Maundy Thursday, Good Friday, and Holy Saturday, the word *now* is inserted, so that the collect ends:

> "Jesus ... who now lives and reigns with you and the Holy Spirit, one God ..."

I assume this is done to focus our attention on the fact that, even as we remember the arrest and crucifixion of the physical Jesus on earth, he truly is now seated at the right hand of God the Father in heaven.

In other places, the formula is varied to include the phrase, "in the unity of the Holy Spirit," referring to the unifying role of the Spirit within the Trinitarian Godhead.

Examples of this variation are found in the collects for the fourth Sunday of Advent, the first and second Sunday after Christmas, and the fifth and eighth Sunday after the Epiphany (BCP, pp. 212–217).

---

[32] For example, the Collect for the Epiphany, BCP, p. 214.

Another common prayer-ending is some form of the following:

> Through Jesus Christ our Lord, to whom, with you
> and the Holy Spirit be honor and glory.[33]

One possible explanation of this variation is that the collect(s) that conclude with this wording acknowledge some special role or power of God intended to evoke in the worshipper a heightened sense of awe for divine qualities deserving of increased "honor and glory."

The collects at the prayers (to be used to conclude forms I–V of the prayers of the people), found on pages 394–395, end in one of two ways:

- Either in a simple ascription to the Son, e.g., "through (Jesus) Christ our Lord," or with a variation of that singular address (like "for the sake of your Son Jesus Christ our Lord");
- Or in the longer Trinitarian formulary (in collects 5, 6, and 8). The concluding phrase for Collect Number 8 (BCP, p. 395) is an interesting further exception in that it ends, "We ask this for the sake of Jesus Christ, in whom all our intercessions are acceptable through the Spirit, and who lives and reigns for ever and ever."

In short, however, collects and other prayers in *The Book of Common Prayer* will typically end with some version of the Trinitarian formulary that includes the Holy Spirit within the Trinitarian profession of "one God."

---

[33] For example, the Collect for the Third Sunday of Advent, BCP, p. 212.

The Daily Office(s)

Outside the collects and prayers, the Gloria Patria ("Glory to the Father, and to the Son, and to the Holy Spirit") is used in the daily offices at the conclusion of the Psalm(s), and in similar forms at the end of certain canticles (e.g., BCP, pp. 49–52).

The Eucharistic Canon(s)

There are eight Eucharistic Canons in the BCP, all of which end with some form of the Trinitarian formulary. Presumably, because of slight intentional differences of focus, each of the eight Trinitarian endings is slightly different:

> Holy Eucharist, Rite I, p.336 and 343, reads: "By whom, and with whom, in the unity of the Holy Ghost, all honor and glory be unto thee, O Father Almighty, world without end."

> Holy Eucharist, Rite II, Eucharistic Prayer A, p. 363, reads: " ... through your Son Jesus Christ. By him, and with him and in him, in the unity of the Holy Spirit all honor and glory is yours, Almighty Father."

Holy Eucharist, Rite II, Eucharistic Prayer B, p. 369, reads: "... through Jesus Christ our Lord, the first born of all creation, the head of the Church, the author of our salvation. By him and with him and in him, in the unity of the Holy Spirit all honor and glory is yours, Almighty Father."

Holy Eucharist, Rite II, Eucharistic Prayer C, p. 372, reads: "... Accept these prayers, Father, through Jesus Christ our great High Priest, to whom with you and the Holy Spirit, your Church gives honor, glory and worship, from generation to generation."

Holy Eucharist, Rite II, Eucharistic Prayer D, p. 375, reads: "Through Christ, and with Christ, and in Christ, all honor and glory are yours, Almighty God and Father, in the unity of the Holy Spirit, for ever and ever."

In the section of the Prayer Book titled Communion under Special Circumstances are found two additional Eucharistic canons:

Form 1 (BCP pp. 402–403) ends with the words: "Gather us by this Holy Communion into one body in your Son Jesus Christ ... By him, and with him, and in him, in the unity of the Holy Spirit all honor and glory is yours, Almighty Father, now and forever."

Form 2 (BCP pp. 404–405) concludes: "All this we ask through your Son Jesus Christ. By him, and with him, and in him, in the unity of the Holy Spirit all honor and glory is yours, Almighty Father, now and forever."

THE PASTORAL OFFICES

Marriage (BCP p. 428): "I pronounce that they are husband and wife, in the Name of the Father, and of the Son, and of the Holy Spirit."

The final petition in the prayers (BCP, p. 430) says: "... on earth as it is in heaven; where, O Father, with your Son and the Holy Spirit, you live and reign in perfect unity ..."

Thanksgiving for a child (BCP p. 445): "May God the Father, who by Baptism adopts us as his children, grant you grace ... May God the Son, who sanctified a home at Nazareth, fill you with love ... May God the Holy Spirit, who has made the Church one family, keep you in peace ..."

Reconciliation (BCP pp. 448, 451): The absolution is pronounced "in the Name of the Father, and of the Son, and of the Holy Spirit."

Ministration to the sick (BCP p. 455): The laying on of hands and anointing is administered "[Through]

Jesus Christ [our Lord], who lives and
reigns with you and the Holy Spirit, one
God …"

Ministration at the time of death (BCP p. 462f.): In addition to
the Trinitarian formulary at the end of
most of the prayers, the commendation
at the time of death reads as follows
(BCP p. 464):

Depart, O Christian soul, out of this world;
In the Name of God the Father Almighty who
created you;
In the Name of Jesus Christ who redeemed you;
In the Name of the Holy Spirit who sanctifies you.
May your rest be this day in peace, and your dwelling
place in the Paradise of God.

Burial office(s) (Rite I, BCP pp. 469–489 and Rite II, pp.
491–505): Except for the use of the
Trinitarian formulary to conclude
the opening collect(s) and on the
final petition of the prayers, all else
(Proper Preface, Commendation, The
Committal and all but one of the
Additional Prayers) is offered "to God,"
"through Jesus Christ." This is most
likely because it is the resurrected Christ
and his mediating function that alone
makes it possible for believers to enter
into their eternal inheritance. While this
may seem to some to be a *hairsplitting*

distinction, it is consistent with Pauline theology (Ephesians 1:13–14) in which "the Holy Spirit ... is the guarantee of our inheritance *until we acquire it.*" [emphasis added]

THE EPISCOPAL OFFICES

The empowering work of the Holy Spirit is abundantly included and invoked in all of the Episcopal offices. However, for the purposes of this chapter, the only point I feel the need to make is that standard forms of the Trinitarian formulary are used consistently in both the prayers and blessings of these offices.

Conclusion

The last issue that needs inclusion in this chapter on basic Trinitarian belief is the question of *why* it is important to consider Trinitarian belief as foundational within Episcopal belief and worship. I would like to suggest four reasons:

> First, to establish that Episcopal belief about the Trinity (and the role of the Holy Spirit) is solidly within the boundaries of orthodox Christian belief.

> Second, assuming interaction between the three persons of the Trinity shows the relational nature of our God and thus, the importance to God of connection, interaction, and relationship. If we were to look at only one place in Scripture, however, where we find support for this statement, it would probably

be in John, chapter 17, verses 21–22, wherein Jesus prays that his followers will "be one even as you [Father] and I [Jesus] are one … perfectly one."

Third, recognizing that the creator God, the Father, is (in the words of the prophet Isaiah, Isaiah 6:1): "High and lifted up and his train fills the temple," and that Jesus, the Son, is now "seated at the right hand of God" (see Colossians 3:1), in order for there to be a person of the Trinity interacting with and available to individual believers and to the churc then it *must* be the role and function of the Holy Spirit (see John 14:17). One of the titles that Jesus gives to the Holy Spirit when he speaks about the Spirit in the Gospel of John is Paraclete (in Greek, *parakletos*, parakhtos), which literally means, "the one called alongside of."

Fourth, one function of the Holy Spirit in the process of interacting with and being available to believers and the church is the function of empowerment (see Luke 4:14 and Romans 15:13, and elsewhere in the New Testament).

SUMMARY

To this point, I have attempted to show that Episcopal Christian worship, as found in the offices of the BCP, solidly holds to the orthodox Christian belief in a triune God, and that (as examples from every division of the BCP were intended to show) the Holy Spirit is included as a coequal member of the Trinitarian Godhead.

This including of the Holy Spirit is expressed both in the simplest form of Trinitarian language in the prayer book, the Trinitarian formulary (i.e., "Father, Son, and Holy Spirit, one God"), as well as in variations of this simple formulation.

Questions for Personal Reflection and/or Group Discussion

1. If a member of a group like the Jehovah's Witnesses told you that the Trinity is not mentioned in the Bible, what would you say in response?

2. Comment on the equality of the three persons of the Godhead. Why might this be considered important?

3. List some ways that you think relationships between Christians are important. What does your awareness of the

relationship and interaction between the three persons of the Trinity suggest to you about relationship between Christians?

4. What does it mean to you when you hear the Holy Spirit referred to as the Paraclete? When have you been aware of the Holy Spirit "coming alongside of" you?

5. How, in your opinion, could the church be more effective in its work if more attention were devoted to invoking the empowerment of the Holy Spirit?

APPENDIX B

Holy Ghost versus Holy Spirit

In simplest terms, Holy Ghost is seen as an archaism, in the same way that the terms thee, thy, thou, etc. are generally seen by contemporary Americans.

Furthermore, mostly as a result of movies, TV shows, novels, etc., the term *ghost* has come to be more associated with an apparition, a visible appearance of a deceased person to the living. To use the term *Holy Ghost*, therefore, could have the tendency to suggest that the third person of the Trinity is not a constant and permanent persona of God, but merely a *specter*.

Some other world religions hold to the idea of avatars—divine beings appearing in human form. Use of the term *Holy Ghost* could further muddle understanding if the term *ghost* was seen by some as an avatar of God rather than a real, constant, and permanent manifestation of God's presence in the world.

Therefore, it has become customary, at least among most Episcopal Christians, to prefer use of the term *Holy Spirit* as a way of avoiding the possible confusions as explained above.

APPENDIX C

The Use and Placement of the Epiclesis in Sacramental Rites Other than Baptism and the Holy Eucharist

Other Sacramental Rites

In our tradition, only two sacraments are recognized (Holy Baptism and Holy Communion). In addition, there are five other sacramental rites mentioned in the Catechism (*The American Book of Common Prayer,* page 860). They are:

1. Confirmation
2. Ordination
3. Holy Matrimony
4. Reconciliation of a Penitent
5. Unction of the Sick

Of these five sacramental rites, only one, Unction of the Sick, includes an invocation of the Holy Spirit as the power to sanctify the sacramental element which, in the case of unction, is the oil.

Unction of the Sick

And, in this rite, it only occurs in the prayer for the blessing of the oil (BCP, p. 455) used for anointing the sick. The priest is directed to say:

> "O Lord, Holy Father, giver of health and salvation: send your Holy Spirit to sanctify this oil ... that those who in faith and repentance receive this holy unction [may] be made whole."[34]

The priest's prayer calls upon God to send the Holy Spirit to act upon the oil of unction in the same way he acted upon the water for baptism and acted upon the bread and wine of Holy Communion, changing it into a "certain means of grace," a channel through which the grace of God (in this case, grace for healing and wholeness) can be carried to the believer and united with the faith of the one standing in eager anticipation of receiving wholeness from God.

---

[34] In my experience, the bishop usually has a special service for the blessing of the oil of unction, and he or she is the one (not a priest) who prays for the blessing of the oil.

APPENDIX D

Other Examples of the Transformative Functions of the Holy Spirit

Other examples of the use of the word *sanctify*:

BCP p. 100, Morning Prayer II: Collect for Mission

BCP pp. 206, 256, Collect #15 (III): For all Christians in their vocations.

BCP p. 278, The Solemn Collects for Good Friday: "By whose Spirit the whole body of your faithful people is governed and sanctified."

BCP p. 148, The Great Litany: "O God the Holy Ghost, Sanctifier of the faithful"

BCP p. 369, Holy Eucharist II—Eucharistic Prayer B: "Unite us to your Son in his sacrifice that we may be acceptable through him, being sanctified by the Holy Spirit."

BCP p. 374, Holy Eucharist II—Eucharistic Prayer D:

"That we might live no longer for ourselves, but for him who died and rose for us, he sent the Holy Spirit ... to bring to fulfillment the sanctification of all."

Other examples of the use of the phrase *to amend our lives*:

BCP p. 152, The Great Litany: "That it may please thee to ... endue us with the grace of thy Holy Spirit to amend our lives."

BCP p. 550, Litany for Ordinations: "For ourselves, for the forgiveness of our sins, and for the grace of the Holy Spirit to amend our lives."

Other examples emphasize the role of "the Holy Spirit ... to *make us holy*":

BCP p. 269, The Absolution after the Litany of Penitence for Ash Wednesday: "Therefore, we beseech him to grant us true repentance and his Holy Spirit ... that the rest of our life hereafter may be pure and holy."

BCP p. 481, The prayers in Burial Rite I ask God to: "Grant us who are still in our pilgrimage ... that thy Holy Spirit may lead us in holiness and righteousness all our days."

Other examples of the *renewing* of the Holy Spirit:

BCP pp. 161, 213, Second Collect for Christmas Day: "Grant that we ... may daily be renewed by thy Holy Spirit."

Other examples of calling on the Holy Spirit to *strengthen*:

> BCP p. 226, Collect for Seventh Sunday of Easter: "Send us your Holy Spirit to strengthen us."

> BCP p. 311, Collect for ending Baptism when there is no Eucharist: "Almighty God ... grant you to be strengthened with might by his Holy Spirit."

> BCP p. 418, Words that may be used by a bishop at confirmation: "Strengthen, O Lord, your servant N. with your Holy Spirit."

> BCP p. 420, Prayer in A Form of Commitment to Christian Service: "May the Holy Spirit guide and strengthen you that ... you may do God's will."

> BCP p. 460, A Collect for Health of Body and Soul: "May God the Father bless you, God the Son heal you, and God the Holy Spirit give you strength."

> BCP p. 460, A Collect for Doctors and Nurses: "Strengthen them by your life-giving Spirit, that by their ministries the health of the community may be promoted."

> BCP p. 819, A Collect for Those about to Be Baptized: "Make the hearts of your servants ready to receive the blessing of the Holy Spirit, that they may be filled with the strength of his presence."

> BCP p. 860, The Catechism: Other Sacramental Rites:

"Confirmation is the rite in which we express a mature commitment to Christ and receive strength from the Holy Spirit through prayer and the laying on of hands by a bishop"

The only example of a connection between the Holy Spirit and the word *empower* is found in the bishop's words used at confirmation (BCP, pp. 418 and 309).

Other examples of the use of the word *sustain* in conjunction with the Holy Spirit:

> BCP p. 308, Concluding Collect in Holy Baptism: "By water and the Holy Spirit you have bestowed upon these your servants the forgiveness of sins, and have raised them to the new life of grace. Sustain them, O Lord, in your Holy Spirit."

> BCP pp. 309, 418, Confirmation: "*Strengthen* ... with your Holy Spirit ... and sustain him/her all the days of his/her life."

> BCP p. 549, Litany for Ordinations: "That by the indwelling of the Holy Spirit he/she may be *sustained and encouraged* to persevere to the end."

Other examples of the Holy Spirit connected with the word *uphold*:

> BCP pp. 310, 419, This is the sentence used by the bishop in re-affirmation: "N., may the Holy Spirit, who has begun a good work in you, direct and uphold you in the service of Christ."

Other examples of the Holy Spirit as the agent by which we are drawn *closer to God*:

> BCP p. 569, Consecration of a church: "Holy Spirit, open our eyes, our ears, our hearts, that we may grow closer to you through joy and through suffering."

Other examples of the Holy Spirit being asked to give *comfort*:

> BCP pp. 175, 227, Second Collect for the Day of Pentecost: "O God, who on this day taught the hearts of your faithful people by sending to them the light of your Holy Spirit; Grant us by the same Spirit to … evermore rejoice in his holy comfort."

> BCP p. 128, Absolution in Compline: "May the Almighty God grant us forgiveness of all our sins, and the grace and comfort of the Holy Spirit."

> BCP p. 107, Concluding prayers in the Order of Service for Noonday: "Heavenly Father, send your Holy Spirit into our hearts … to comfort us in all our afflictions."

There are no other examples of the Holy Spirit being asked to give *consolation*.

Other examples of the Holy Spirit being asked to give *guidance*:

> BCP p. 420, A Form of Commitment to Christian Service: "May the Holy Spirit guide and strengthen you … that … you may do God's will."

BCP p. 513, The Presentation in the Ordination of a Bishop: "N., Bishop in the Church of God, the clergy and people of the Diocese of N., trusting in the guidance of the Holy Spirit have chosen ..."

BCP p. 832, Collect for Guidance #58: "O God, by whom the meek are guided in judgment ... Grant us ... that the Spirit of wisdom may save us from all false choices."

Other examples of the Holy Spirit being asked to *give direction*:

BCP p. 107, Prayers at Noonday: "Heavenly Father, send your Holy Spirit into our hearts to direct and rule us according to your will."

BCP pp. 310, 418, Words spoken by the bishop in reaffirmation: "N., may the Holy Spirit, who has begun a good work in you, direct and uphold you in the service of Christ."

Other examples of the Holy Spirit being asked to *lead us into all truth:*

BCP pp. 348, 381, Proper Preface for Baptism: "Because in Jesus Christ our Lord you have received us as your sons and daughters, made us citizens of your kingdom, and given us the Holy Spirit to guide us into all truth."

BCP p. 815, Prayer for All Sorts and Conditions of Men #2: "We pray for thy holy Church universal; that it may be so guided and governed by thy good Spirit, that all who profess and call themselves Christians may be led into the way of truth."

BCP p. 852, Catechism: How is the Holy Spirit revealed in the New Covenant? "The Holy Spirit is revealed as the Lord who leads us into truth."

Other examples of the Holy Spirit being asked to rule and govern:

BCP pp. 57, 100, Morning Prayer I and II Collect for Guidance and Prayer for Mission: "We humbly pray you so to guide and govern us by your Holy Spirit."

"Almighty and everlasting God, by whose Spirit the whole body of your faithful people is governed and sanctified." (Also, p. 278, Good Friday Solemn Collects)

BCP p. 815, Prayer for All Sorts and Conditions of men: #2: "We pray for thy holy Church universal; that it may be so guided and governed by thy good Spirit, that all who profess and call themselves Christians may be led into the way of truth."

CONCLUSION

The purpose of this book has been threefold:

1. To acquaint (especially) Episcopal laypeople with the manifold and varied works of the Holy Spirit, not only in the Liturgies we use for worship, but also in baptism and the Holy Eucharist;
2. To familiarize all Christian laypeople with the ways in which the Holy Spirit has been made available to us for a large variety of purposes, generally for personal transformation and for empowerment in mission and ministry;
3. And to make laypeople aware of the rich assortment of prayers that can be used in personal devotions, as well as public worship, to invoke the Holy Spirit to enrich and energize every facet of our individual and common life and ministry.

I hope by including the questions for study, reflection, and discussion that the usefulness of this book will be in the area of application to life and not just the accumulation of new information.

It has been my fervent hope and prayer since beginning the writing of these pages that if enough laypeople read and take to heart their contents, our wonderful Episcopal Church can and will be renewed and strengthened to be the shining star our Lord intends it to be.

I am grateful to all the readers who have *hung in there* with me to the culmination of the ideas and examples in these pages. But more importantly, I hope that the readers' feel their time was well spent and that some useful tools have been gained.

Collect of the Holy Spirit (BCP, p. 251):

Almighty and most merciful God, grant that by the indwelling of your Holy Spirit we may be enlightened and strengthened for your service; through Jesus Christ our Lord, who lives and reigns with you, in the unity of the Holy Spirit, one God, now and forever. Amen.

References

Dreyer, Elizabeth A. *Holy Power, Holy Presence.* Mahwah, NJ: Paulist Press, 2007.

Griffiss, James E. *The Anglican Vision.* The New Church's Teaching Series, vol. 1. Boston: Cowley Publications, 1997.

Hughes, Robert Davis III, "The Holy Spirit in Christian Spirituality." *The Blackwell Companion to Christian Spirituality,* ed. Arthur Holder, New York: Wiley-Blackwell Publishing, 2005.

_____ *Beloved Dust.* New York and London: Continuum Publishing Group, 2008.

Malcolm, Lois. *Holy Spirit: Creative Power in Our Lives.* Minneapolis, Minnesota: Augsburg Press, 2009.

Stevick, Daniel B. *Baptismal Moments, Baptismal Meanings.* Chicago: Church Hymnal Corp., Inc., 1988.

_____ *By Water and the Word: the Scriptures of Baptism.* New York: Church Publishing, Inc., 1997.

Westerhoff, John H. *Will Our Children Have Faith?* New York: Seabury Press, 1976.

INDEX

CPSIA information can be obtained
at www.ICGtesting.com
Printed in the USA
FFOW05n0009020415